The Profitmover's Guide to Business Success

BY

James B. Larsen

Hara Publishing
P.O. Box 19732
Seattle, Washington

The Profitmover's Guide
to Business Success

Applause for
The Profitmover's Guide to Business Success

"If I hadn't hired Jim Larsen and applied his business and financial recommendations, my company would not be in business today!"
— *John Chipman,* The Chipman Company

"By using the *Profitmover* guide we increased our bottom line from 2% to 7% in the first year!"
— *Hal Morrell,* Bailey's Moving and Storage

"We were in real trouble when Jim Larsen walked into our company. By applying the principles he outlined and got us to focus on, we became profitable."
— *Rick Anderson,* Armstrong Moving and Storage

"Our company has worked with Jim Larsen for over 10 years, and without a doubt, he has not only helped us to be profitable, but has guided us through some very trying times."
— *Gerard Barrieau,* Barrieau Moving and Storage

"With the untimely passing of my father, I inherited his position as President/CEO of our company. With Jim Larsen's guidance and by applying the principles outlined in the *Profitmover* guide, we are now a successful and profitable company."
— *Joe Harris,* Harris Moving and Storage

"We were in deep trouble financially when we hired Jim Larsen. He immediately went to work by getting myself and all our managers to apply the basic rules of running a business as outlined in his book The Profitmover's Guide to Business Success. If you're in trouble financially, I can't think of a better book to read or a better person than Jim Larsen to help you out."
— *Steve Herman*, A Action, Inc.

"I first met Jim Larsen when I hired him to help our company handle and solve some unique transportation challenges. Jim worked with our company for over 15 years and did an outstanding job. I highly recommend his new book *The Profitmover's Guide to Business Success.*
— *James Schlueter, Retired*
Consolidated Freightways

Acknowledgements

Every author is indebted to the influences that have shaped his thoughts and habits. I would like to express and acknowledge those individuals most responsible for this book.

First, I would like to thank all the CEO's and managers I have worked with over the past 15 years, (some 700 companies) who have shared with me their concerns and successes in running their businesses. The education and knowledge I acquired from these individuals has been invaluable and helped me to write this book.

Secondly, I want to thank Thorn Bacon who edited this book. His insight and editorial expertise helped shape this book into a modern business text that became easy but valuable reading for anyone wanting to improve their company.

Thirdly, I want to thank Mike Larsen and David Borgwardt who followed and tested the recommendations outlined in this book, proving that exceptional profits can be made by following the basic steps for running a business successfully as outlined in this book.

Fourth, I want to thank and express my appreciation to all the controllers and accountants that I have worked with either turning a company around or helping to enhance its profitability. At times I pushed hard for proper detail, but in most cases they came through with the financial detail needed to make decisions for change that would help their company to become financially successful. Their help gave me great insights in writing this book.

Fifth, I want to thank Mimi McGee for helping in typing and re-typing the total text of this book. Her contributions helped move this book to a successful conclusion.

Lastly, I would like to thank my wonderful wife, Linda, for her consistent support.

All of the above mentioned people have helped me to produce this book and the success of this project is attributable to their involvement and contributions.

Table of Contents

Introduction

I could start out this introduction by asking the question: "Who should read this book?" My answer would be, "Anyone who cares about making a profit!" Everyone in business wants to make a profit. The difference between the wish and the reality of it happening comes down to a number of actions that must take place consistently. These necessary actions and consistent decisions are explained in this book.

I have had the wonderful opportunity of working with more than 700 companies to help them realize profit and in doing so, have seen the very best and worst run organizations. Unfortunately Prado's Law is the general rule that applies to profit success: only about 20 percent of the companies in business have organizations that function properly and the other 80 percent suffer from a complete lack of organization and just hope that profit will happen.

In today's market, competition is fierce on every front! Price is an issue for almost every transaction and customers want, and expect, more service. With these changes and pressures taking place, successful companies are required to have efficient working systems that measure and re-evaluate all areas of the organization so that meaningful changes can be made.

Good management is the key to making profits happen in a company. It is incumbent upon management to take a hard look at what they are doing in all areas, and, when necessary, make changes that will keep their business on course. In my opinion, companies whose management works diligently at sales and financial organization will succeed, and those who do not will eventually fail!

In this book, there are 35 chapters which deal with almost every facet of running a business profitably. Each chapter title asks a pertinent question which is answered in the text that follows.

I have written this book to help companies become more professional at operating their businesses. It will help provoke thought and develop new ideas for your company which will lead to a stronger bottom line.

Profit is the

Result of

Many Positive Actions!

We Succeed Only if We Make a Profit!

We Must Have a Goal That States:
We are Here to Make
as Much Money as We Can.

You Must Believe This if You Want Good Profits!

The Correct Definition of Management

is Getting Work Done

Efficiently and Productively

Through the Efforts of Others.

Profit Isn't An End In Itself,

It's The Beginning!

The Mechanics
of Running a Business
are Really Not Very Complicated
When it Gets Down to Essentials.

To be Successful
You Have to Sell Your Products
or Services to Someone
for More Than They Cost You to Produce.

Chapter One

Are You a *Profitmover*?

Profits are absolutely essential for your business to be successful! Without profits your company will eventually fail. So profits are of the utmost importance. Being a *Profitmover* means that you will move in as many different directions as necessary and make as many changes as necessary to develop the goals you have set for your company. Profit therefore, is a crucial objective that you must accomplish to make your goals come true.

To be an outstanding *Profitmover* means that first and foremost as CEO, manager, or owner you must have an absolute commitment to making a profit. You must demonstrate your commitment to all employees by showing them that you are continually focused, persistent and consistent, tough minded when necessary, and fair in your zeal to obtain your profit goal.

It has been my experience as a consultant on profitmaking to more than 700 companies that most CEOs, managers or owners establish a profit goal via a budget or business plan, but they do not understand what needs to be changed or made different in their operation during the year to accomplish that goal. If business is conducted in the same way as it was the year before, how can the results be expected to be any different?

The true *Profitmover* is the executive who understands the importance of all areas - - - sales, operations, accounting, human relations, public relations, and others, and is able to blend them together so they all work effectively to support the main cause of the business - - - making a profit. This may seem to be an obvious objective, but it is surprising how many companies in dozens of fields seem to forget how important profit is to the health of the business. Without consistent profit a company will fail.

One of the most important things a *Profitmover* can do is to get everyone to work toward being the best. If the employees believe they are the best, the company becomes the best, and when this happens employees are excited about coming to work and will help produce better results for the bottom line. The *Profitmover* makes every employee understand that he or she is important and is part of the total process of being profitable. When they understand how their job fits into the total equation of making money, they get excited. Being the best involves six key processes. They are:

1. Change is required. Always look for better ways and processes to improve the company.

2. Train and educate. The best-educated and trained employees are happier and produce more.
3. Set standards and benchmarks for every employee, not just managers. An employee, who understands what is expected of him in his job, is one who will attain or beat the benchmarks.
4. Reward and compliment people who produce or contribute the most. When employees know they will be compensated for a stronger effort, they produce more.
5. Develop a company-wide mindset that works at quality, with a total commitment to strong customer service.
6. Make sure everyone in your organization understands that each is responsible for the company being profitable. Show them by benchmarks how they can be strong contributors to the company's prosperity and to their own.

If you want to attain strong profits in your company you must apply the above-mentioned principles consistently!

Chapter Two

Can You Pass the *Profitmover* Test?

Thoughtfully answering the questions in this test can be the most important action you can initiate to measure the profitmaking health of your company.

And now that the importance of making profit has been firmly established, let's determine how your company rates on the success scale of profitmakers. The following test will not only help you evaluate how your company stands, but what areas need improvement. Circle Yes or No and if you don't understand the question, read the chapter listed in the Table of Contents that corresponds to the question.

Chapter	Question	Answer	Points
3	*Are You Managing Your Company Effectively?* (Do you put a plan in place everyday that causes you to focus on profit enhancement?)	Y N	____
4	*Do Your Sales Drive Profitable Revenues?* (Do you control prices for your services and products by means of a written pricing policy?)	Y N	____
5	*Do Your Salespeople Understand The Importance Of Selling Added Value?* (Do you educate and train your salespeople to sell added value?)	Y N	____
6	*Are You Sure You Are Pricing Your Products And Services Properly So A Profit Is Realized?* (Do you know your sales cost, labor cost, overhead cost, facilities cost, risk cost, equipment cost, and materials cost so that you can price your service and product properly?)	Y N	____
7	*Are You Costing For Profits?* (Do you understand and know the effects that business mix, productivity, capacity, and quality can have on your pricing?)	Y N	____

8   *Do You Know Your Allocations And Cost Accounting?*   Y N   _____
        (Do you know and have a proper allocation of fixed
        and variable costs?)

9   *Do You Know What Cost Of Sale Is?*   Y N   _____
        (Do you have a costing method that can tell you the
        cost of sales by individual salesperson and total company?)

10 *Do You Know Your Overhead Costs?*   Y N   _____
        (Do you know what your overhead costs are as a
        percent of revenue?)

11 *Do You Know Your Labor Costs?*   Y N   _____
        (Do you have labor costing that can tell you what
        your fully loaded hourly costs are by employee?)

12 *Are You Controlling Supplies And Material Cost?*   Y N   _____
        (Do you have procedures that can tell you daily what
        your status is regarding inventory?)

13 *Do You Understand Risk Costs?*   Y N   _____
        (Do you have a claims tracking system that can tell
        you what the cost of claims is by type of revenue?)

14 *Do You Understand Your Equipment Costs?*   Y N   _____
        (Do you have a costing method that can tell you how
        to allocate the cost of equipment to a given line of
        revenue?)

15 *Do You Understand And Know Your Plant Or*
     Warehouse Cost?   Y N   _____
        (Do you have a costing method for allocating space costs?)

16 *Have You Established Productivity Standards And*
     Benchmarks For Every Employee In Your Company?   Y N   _____
        (Do you have a system that develops proper
        standards and benchmarks for your employees?)

17 *Can You Pass The Company Analysis?*   Y N   _____
        (Do you know exactly where your company stands
        financially at any given time?)

18 *Do You Understand And Know What Big Questions To*
     Ask When Analyzing Your Financial Statement?   Y N   _____
        (Do you have a financial analysis process that tells
        you whether you are on plan and if not, what needs
        to be fixed to get back on track?)

19 *Are You Controlling Your Credit?*   Y N   ____
(Do you have a written credit policy that all of your
employees understand and follow?)

20 *How Good Are You At Collecting Your Receivables?*   Y N   ____
(Do you have strong collection goals that are
adhered to and which maintain good cash flow?)

21 *Do You Work At Increasing Cash Flow?*   Y N   ____
(Do you follow strong cash flow procedures that
increase your cash flow?)

22 *How Is Your Cash Flow?*   Y N   ____
(Does your company have a positive cash flow? Are
you in the preferred position?)

23 *Do You Budget?*   Y N   ____
(Do you establish an annual budget plan for your
company and do a budget deviation analysis each month?)

24 *Are Financial Ratios Important To Running Your Business?*   Y N   ____
(Do you look at and use financial ratios in running
your business?

25 *Do You Know Your Break-even?*   Y N   ____
(Do you pull and update the break-even on your
company monthly?)

26 *Do You Have Order Control?*   Y N   ____
(Can you account for every order in a month via
a computer order entry system?)

27 *Are You Hiring Right?*   Y N   ____
(Do you have a formal step-by-step hiring system that
will help you to find the right person for the right job?)

28 *Are You Training And Educating Enough?*   Y N   ____
(Do you have a formal training program in place
that can help your employees be more productive?)

29 *Is Quality Important?*   Y N   ____
(Do you work diligently at developing a strong
quality program that focuses on zero defect?)

30 *Are You Watching Your Business Mix?*   Y N   ____
(Do you have an analysis process in place that will
help you add a profitable mix of business?)

31 *Do You Have The Big Five Support?*   Y N   ____
     (Do you have a strong business relationship with
     your CPA, Banker, Lawyer, Insurance Agent and
     Computer Consultant?)

32 *Do You Have A Profitmover Plan?*   Y N   ____
     (When you come in each morning is there a written
     plan of action that you follow?

33 *Do You Have An Exit Plan?*   Y N   ____
     (Have you put in place an exit plan that will take care
     of you in retirement and still keep the company
     financially strong?)

34 *Will You Change?*   Y N   ____
     (Are you willing to make change daily that will
     enhance the profitability of your company?)

Total Score _____

Scoring the Profitmover Test

To find your total score, add up all the Yes answers and multiply by 3. Add up your points and compare the total to the levels listed below to determine your business health.

0 to 30 Points: *Your Company Is Financially Weak and In the Emergency Alert Status.*
                 Hire a turnaround expert!

31 to 60 Points: *Your Company Is Financially Fair.*
                 When you score in this range you have some serious problems which
                 need attention. Have your management team discuss the issues raised
                 by this test with the purpose of formulating corrective and immediate
                 action. If proper solutions can't be found, hire outside help.

61 to 102 Points: *Your Company Is Financially Strong and Operating Well.*
                 You still need to be vigilant by staying on top of all aspects of profit-
                 making as outlined in test.

Now that you have discovered the strength and weakness of your company based on the number of points you scored on the test, the next step for you is to answer the questions, Am I managing my company effectively? How can I improve? These two questions are addressed in the next chapter.

If you answered the questions on the *Profitmover Test* honestly and did not qualify your responses, then unless your company ranks among the 20 percent in the nation that produces 80 percent of all the profits made in business, you know you have improvements to make. The sooner you decide to implement changes, the sooner your profit line will begin to move upward.

An excerpt from a statement made on page 7 in Chapter One bears repeating here because the story that follows is about the chief executive of a young company and it will have great relevance to the question Are You A Profitmover?

Here is the excerpt:

The true Profitmover is the executive who understands the importance of all areas— sales, operations, accounting, human relations, public relations and others, and is able to blend them together so they all work effectively to support the main cause of the business— making a profit.

Certainly, that was the objective of Ralph Barnes (not his real name), a 32-year-old with a doctorate in health management who was president of an organization that sold health promotion models to corporations interested in improving their profits by providing better working environments and condition for their employees.

As the chief salesman for his company, Ralph had no equal. He traveled extensively, making up to 150 presentations yearly around the country of his company's health promotion models to groups of corporations that attended his seminars.

His delivery was eloquent. His message backed up with pertinent facts and figures, was strongly convincing and his enrollment record of new customers signing up for his products or services was more than outstanding. In the first two years in his role of chief executive, the company's profits soared, but began to decline in the third year.

What happened to this marvel of sales and persuasion? It is an old story and it still happens with surprising regularity. Many companies permit their star player, performing so brilliantly, to fail to delegate important responsibilities, and develop a support staff that can implement the rewards and responsibilities of his singular efforts. Stockholders and board members are so dazzled by the mounting sales the CEO is piling up that they forget the cardinal rule of business success–FOLLOW THROUGH.

This was the case with Ralph who saw the need to hire a company to develop a sophisticated package that would tell the success story of his company. Key to the development of the package was the provision that, under his direction, strategic information would be furnished to the sales development firm, necessary for creating the project. And then the trouble began. Ralph seldom returned telephone calls from the company that required his insight. Data requested to provide the building blocks of the sales package arrived late or not at all many times.

Finally, after dozens of delays and unfulfilled promises from Ralph, who was busy traveling and gathering more new business, the company he had hired invoked the cancellation clause in the contract.

Not only had Ralph's company lost its investment of $75,000 with nothing to show for it but along the way discovered that Ralph's inattention to other important customers and providers resulted in significant loss of confidence in the company.

A brilliant sales executive failed to understand the necessity of building a strong support team and delegating responsibilities in an orderly and well-planned fashion.

Surely, you must conclude, the CEO's board of directors counseled with their star player, insisting that he hire a strong assistant who would implement the company strategies necessary to build an effective administrative support team to follow through on their CEO's commitments.

As a matter of fact, the board did not act. They did not wish to give Ralph the impression that they disapproved of him.

Failure to change when it is necessary for profits and survival is one of the most common errors of companies in America. And my own experience as a consultant is that the majority of those executives who diligently answered the questions in the *Profitmover's Test* in Chapter II, failed to inact the changes recommended in order to improve profits.

The last impression I wish to give in this book is that I am a know-it-all who has all the answers. Certainly that is not true. What is absolutely true is an amusing statement that sums up the financial conditions of thousands of companies in the United States—"We are a non-profit organization. We didn't mean to be, but we are."

That situation can change if you are willing to follow the recommendations in this book which have increased the bottom line for companies I have consulted for and who have put to use the information contained in these pages.

Chapter Three

Am I Managing My Company Effectively?

Working with different owners, managers and CEOs over the past fifteen years, I have found that many of them do not really understand how to manage a company. They come into work without the foggiest idea of what they should be doing on that day. There is no plan or list of priorities established that leads them into an orderly process of management. In other words, they do what happens, not what is planned.

When I confront a common situation like this, I first say, "Show me how you manage." Invariably the answer is, "What do you mean?" I reply, "I'm looking for a daily process, or program you use to inform you how well your company is doing daily and month-to-date". Few managers I've met have such an important asset. Most managers don't have any daily plan that tells them how the company is doing month-to-date. Instead they just work on what comes to mind or crosses their desk. With such a haphazard approach to profitmaking, is it any wonder that their bottom line is suffering?

It became apparent to George, the owner of a trucking company primarily engaged in moving household goods, that there must be something wrong with his style of business management when he scored in the low fifties on the *Profitmover* test. He was quite disturbed and wanted to take action immediately to remedy his shortcomings.

I agreed to do a management analysis of his company and two weeks later I delivered a report to him that compared his company financially against his industry's standard of profits. When George saw how poorly his company was performing in comparison with other truckers whose profit picture was far more favorable than his, he resolved to follow the recommendations I had made. But he procrastinated - weeks went by with no action on his part.

Finally, I called him one day and told him that he was wasting his money paying me for recommendations that apparently he did not intend to put into effect. I said the health of his company was deteriorating and that if he was unable to make changes that involved reorganization and termination of five or six employees, then he had better hire someone who could. George finally did hire a manager who came in and cleaned house. As a result the profitability of his company doubled in the first year—from a low two to three percent to seven percent. Following the new management plan, the company achieved fourteen percent the second year.

Like many others with whom I have worked, George had to develop the *Profitmover* mentality. To make this easier for you, you will find a convenient priority list of actions to take to start on the road to increased profits:

1. On the night before, fill out the *Profitmover Priority List* of things to do and accomplish the next day.
2. Give each item a priority, starting with the most important one and proceeding to lesser ones. These priorities would be phone calls, letters, appointments, and things of that nature. The *Profitmover* Daily Planner can assist you.
3. On your list there are certain items that should be fixed and reviewed automatically each day as follows:
    (a) Cash flow report
    (b) Checking account balances
    (c) Revenue billed month-to-date
    (d) Accounts receivable update
    (e) Productivity report
    (f) Number of orders booked-to-date
    (g) Average order value
4. Meet with employees
    (a) Employee reviews on promised review date
    (b) Individual manager updates
    (c) Travel to branches or operations
5. Work on and develop agenda for monthly managers' meetings. Prepare and send out agenda to attendees one week prior to meeting.

I can't leave this chapter without relaying a story that, unhappily, occurs too often in the transportation industry and it illustrates a company that certainly was not managing its affairs effectively and making enemies out of customers. I tell this story to point out what should be an obvious fact: If a customer is treated with courtesy, honesty and with gratitude for the business he has brought to a company, he becomes not only happy with his original decision to hire the company to move his goods, but will spread the word to others. This invisible ripple effect has been calculated in many cases to cause new business to flow in multiples of 400 to 500 percent. The reverse effect can be damaging to a company to a comparable extent.

The unfortunate story of the XYZ company started when a new customer located the mover in the Yellow Pages and a sales representative called to estimate the cost of moving six rooms of furniture. The customer made clear that no packing would be required and no boxes would have to be moved. She had adequate help to move dishes, lamps, clothes, books, paintings and other odds and ends.

The sales representative gave her an estimate of $980 to move the furniture to the new residence seven miles away. The customer paid the requested down payment of $100 and the date for the move was set. When the moving crew arrived, it was composed of three friendly, talkative and slow young men who spent endless time chatting among themselves clustered around their truck. At other times, they held long-winded planning sessions on how to pack the large moving van. More than 12 smaller pieces of furniture (dining chairs and end tables) previously included in the estimate had already been taken to the new location by the customer in order to expedite the actual move.

The result of the crew's ineptitude delayed the loading by several hours. In response to the customer's complaint by phone about the problem, a moving supervisor arrived and pitched in to help get the furniture into the new house.

During the following week, the customer discovered a shelf missing from a cabinet, a broken frame on an expensive wingback chair and a finishing frame torn from another cabinet. She also discovered that the bill for the move was considerably higher than the estimate (in spite of the additional furniture she had moved herself which had been included in the original estimate), and she had not been credited with her down payment.

When the customer contacted the XYZ Moving Company about filing a damage claim and requesting refund of her overpayment, she was given the runaround. Nobody at the company would give her a satisfactory answer. After more than a dozen phone calls and with her patience running short, she notified the company that the next request for settlement would come from her attorney.

To her, more important than the $400 she demanded, was the complete failure of the company to treat her with courtesy and promptness "They just didn't care," she said. "Do you think I'd recommend them to a friend who had a moving job and asked me about the people I used?"

It is obvious from this story that the manager of the XYZ Moving Company was not handling the affairs of his company effectively, and could be losing more customers than acquiring new ones.

Be a ***Profitmover*** and plan the night before.

Profitmover Daily Planner			**Date**
APPOINTMENTS	**Priority**	**TO DO**	**Complete**
7:00			
7:30			
8:00			
8:30			
9:00			
9:30			
10:00			
10:30			
11:00			
11:30			
12:00			
12:30			
1:00			
1:30			
2:00			
2:30			
3:00			
3:30			
4:00			
4:30			
5:00			
5:30			
6:00			
6:30			
Notes			

Profitmover Monthly Planner   Month

Sunday	Monday	Tuesday	Wednesday	Thursday	Friday	Saturday

Notes

Chapter Four

Can You Pass The Sales Team Analysis?

Not too long ago, I saw a cartoon in a magazine that made me chuckle and at the same time made me realize that it expressed the dilemma of sales organizations the world over. The drawing illustrated a sales manager pointing to a red pin on the company's sales territory map. Turning to the worried-looking man beside him he said, "I'm not going to fire you Simmons, but to emphasize the insecurity of your position, I'm going to loosen your pin on our sales map a little."

Someone once said, "Sales are the lifeline of any successful business". I'm sure a salesperson made this statement, and even if it comes from a biased point of view, it has validity. If you don't have orders to manufacture or service, your business will die! So, let's find out how your sales team stacks up.

The following questions and your answers will help to evaluate how your company stands in sales and marketing. Circle Yes or No.

Management Leadership

Yes	No	Can you and your salespeople clearly express your organization's strategic goals and vision?
Yes	No	What is your communication process? Do you hold consistent weekly meetings and provide employee newsletters or internal memos?
Yes	No	Are you and your salespeople active in the business community?
Yes	No	Do you and your salespeople participate on boards or other volunteer activities?
Yes	No	Is the writing of personal, financial and professional goals an annual part of planning for you and your salespeople?
Yes	No	Is there an annual, or more frequent, formal assessment of your business year?
Yes	No	Is there a policy of your salespeople documenting expectations for behaviors and results?
Yes	No	Are the consequences of met or failed mutually agreed-upon expectations discussed?

Sales Process

Yes	No	Do you and your salespeople document key sales processes?
Yes	No	Is prospect and sales-cycle information regularly collected and processed for use?
Yes	No	Are sales plans regularly prepared by each salesperson for his/her territory or assignment?
Yes	No	What process is in place to ensure that all products and services are being promoted to all customers?
Yes	No	Do sales account teams have strategy meetings to share and develop ideas for targeted accounts?
Yes	No	Have you and your salespeople developed a simple way to track sales activities (sales appointments, demos, proposals, and orders)?
Yes	No	Can you obtain key sales data anytime, anywhere, and in a usable format for everyone in your organization via current technology?
Yes	No	Do you educate and train salespeople to sell added value?

Results Management

Yes	No	Do you and your salespeople regularly collect and disseminate results of sales efforts?
Yes	No	Do your salespeople understand the correlation between their sales performance and their compensation?
Yes	No	Do your salespeople receive recognition as a result of their selling efforts?
Yes	No	Is rewarding significant sales results a matter of policy?
Yes	No	Are corrective processes in place signaled by substandard results?
Yes	No	Do your salespeople have a way of determining gross margin on sales they make?

Customer and Market Focus

Yes	No	Is a method in place for consistent gathering of customer requirements?
Yes	No	Is the information provided you by your marketing staff on emerging markets and sales trends timely, as well as useful?
Yes	No	Is an accurate, up-to-date customer database readily available to your sales force electronically?
Yes	No	Is there a viable customer feedback mechanism in place that ensures key changes are implemented?

Human Resources

Yes No Does each position within the organization have clearly defined roles and responsibilities?

Yes No Is your recruiting program thorough and consistent?

Yes No Does everyone on your sales staff really understand the total compensation package—salary, commissions, benefits, stock options, and profit sharing?

Yes No Is an employee survey in place to gauge satisfaction and provide input and feedback?

Professional Growth

Yes No Have you created an environment of trust which values individual contributions and team effort?

Yes No Do you encourage everyone to pursue professional growth and development and provide everyone resources for professional advancement?

Yes No Is productivity a byword in your organization?

Yes No Do you encourage a positive attitude; do your employees like to come to work?

You've been asked 34 questions. Each question answered yes has a value of three, making a total score of 102. Add all the yes answers and multiply by 3. The following point system has been developed to help rate your sales efforts:

0-33 Points: *You Flunk the Test!*
When you score in this range, you do not have a strong and healthy sales team; in fact your sales department is probably the biggest reason you are not making money. Hire someone from the outside to help you get on track immediately!

34-66 Points: *Your Company is Mediocre At Best In It's Ability To Develop Sales.* Your management team needs to go over each question in the questionnaire with the purpose of implementing changes to correct the deficiencies of your present sales team. Failure to do so could mean a slow death for your business.

67-102 Points: **When Your Sales Team Falls In This Range,** You More Than Likely Are Helping The Company To Be Successful. Keep working to stay in this range by continually monitoring where your sales team stands in compliance with the questions in the test. Do not become complacent!

Train and Require Salespeople
to Sell Orders
that are Compensatory

Chapter Five

Do Your Sales Drive Profitable Revenues?

Don't let your salespeople set price! Be sure you have established pricing policies that control what a salesperson can sell a product or service for. To accomplish this you and your employees, and that includes salespeople, must understand the costs involved so you can price your services and products at a profit.

My experience has been that most managers establish a threshold as to how low a salesperson may quote a price and invariably most of them will go directly to the allowed threshold without selling a higher price. Why? Because most companies have not taken the time to train and require salespeople to sell good orders. Very little training, including roll playing, is given on how to sell added value and help the salespeople understand that they have a responsibility to help the company be profitable. There is a saying salespeople use: "Nothing happens until a sale is made". A better way of saying this is: "Nothing *good* happens until a properly priced order is sold".

What kind of sales revenue is your sales department selling?

Profitmovers know!

Customers Will Always Get
What They Want.

The Question is,
"Will They Get it from You?"

Chapter Six

Do Your Salespeople Understand The Importance Of Selling Added Value?

A few years ago, my father-in-law and I were out taking a walk in Saginaw, MI, and ran across a garage sale. We stopped and noticed that there were more than twenty-five books for sale on selling and marketing for 25 cents each. We bought all of them!

One of the books entitled *"Big-League Salesmanship"* by Bert H. Schlain and first published in 1955 (47 years ago) had some real sales gems in it. The one that ties into added value selling is entitled *A Prayer For A Salesman.*

Deliver us from buyers who know the price of everything and the value of nothing; who believe that they can get a dollar's worth for twenty-five cents; who think that cheapness is thrift; who ignore the economy of quality; who believe they are getting something for nothing when they pay less; who buy things just because they are cheap.

We are grateful for customers who realize the extravagance of paying too little; who know the high cost of a low price; who know that somebody is always ready to make things a little worse and sell them a little cheaper.

Salespeople selling in 1955 had the same mentality that salespeople have today, and that is how to sell price rather than added value.

People Don't Buy Price - They Buy Value!
(that is if you sell value)

Understanding Price vs. Value = Cost
Can Mean More Profit

Working with hundreds of companies has brought me to the realization that most are missing the boat by not training salespeople to understand the necessity of selling value.

In the typical scenario, the company informs its salespeople that they can sell at a certain price or discount up to a certain percent to get the order without penalty. What this really means is that salespeople are being allowed to set price, without any knowledge of what the actual cost is for the product or service they are selling. Does this make good business sense?

When salespeople are allowed to establish price in the manner noted above, nine out of ten will present a prospect with the lowest price discount permissible. Most salespeople quote a price, instead of selling the product to a customer. Their mind set is price, price, price, so they open by saying, "Boy, do I have a deal for you. I'm authorized to give you a 45% discount." This is done without even qualifying the prospect's requirements or desires, or whether the company he represents will make a profit. This type of selling is more aptly called order taking, not true salesmanship. From the prospective customer's viewpoint, he or she must be wondering, "How can you discount your sales price by almost 45%, still make money and give excellent service?"

It is a fact that everyone wants a good price, but also everyone wants excellent service and value. It is therefore incumbent upon the true salesperson to be educated and trained in being able to sell added value by understanding the profit equation. To accomplish this the salesperson must understand the following:

1. Realize that the price objection is really the inborn instinct to bargain.
2. When a buyer says, "Your price is too high," he or she is testing to determine the value of the product or service.
3. In the price/value formula, it is important to remember that "value" is the solution you are providing for the buyer to overcome his problems.
4. Recognize that the prospect is working out the formula in his or her mind:

$$\frac{\text{PRICE}}{\text{VALUE}} = \text{COST}$$

Help each prospect work it out. Build up value and lower cost.

5. Remember to sell yourself as part of the package of values.
6. Remember buyers fear cheap service and cheap products.
7. The buyer will always compare your service to a competitor's. Help him work out the price/value and thereby lower cost of your service.
8. Recognize that "Your price is too high," can be a buying signal.

9. By selling added value your closing ratio will be higher.
10. By applying the price/value formula to selling, sales costs are reduced, more sales are made and higher margins are developed, which equates to more profit.

It is important that all salespeople understand, know and be able to sell the added values your company can offer to a customer. A complete list of values should be made up and all salespeople be made to practice, drill and rehearse using them in their presentations to be effective!

Remember the following when selling value:

Step 1 - *Sell the features* and benefits of the product or service and the good character of your company.

Step 2 - Give *proof* = who said so?

Step 3 - Ask for *agreement* = isn't this the kind of service you want?

When asking for agreement you are building toward the close, and when you ask for the order by saying, "Now that we have agreement may I have your order?" Remember to shut up, because the first one to talk loses.

$$\begin{array}{l} \text{PRICE} \\ + \qquad = \text{COST} \\ \text{VALUE} \end{array}$$

I have spent time on this strategy and it works and I cannot emphasize how important it is to the total picture of profitability in a company. If service and products are not sold at a price that allows a proper gross margin, the possibility of profits is nil. **Management and salespeople must know how to sell added value so price is not the only decision the customer has to make to come to a decision to buy. It is the salesperson's responsibility to develop sales that are priced at a level which allows profitability. It is management's responsibility to develop training, education and direction for salespeople so that reasonably priced sales are compensatory for all.**

To be a *Profitmover* selling added value is a must!

Strive to Increase Profits,
Not Just Sales Volume!

Chapter Seven

Are You Sure You Are Pricing Your Products And Services Properly So Profits Are Realized?

One of the first things I discuss with a company is how they price their services and products. Most small companies tell me they price their products based on what they "feel" they're worth. This answer is better known as the seat of the pants guess. Scary! Also, setting price by what your competition sells the product for can get a company into trouble in a hurry. What happens if the competitor's price is wrong or if he has a lower cost than you do? Scary again!

The real answer is to understand all of your costs in such a way that the price reflects a profitable markup. To accomplish this a costing system is needed that indicates what your price should be so a certain margin is obtained to take care of overhead and profit.

The factors that should be included in a cost analysis must include the following:

- Sales cost
- Labor cost
- Overhead cost
- Facilities cost
- Risk cost
- Equipment cost
- Material cost

When you have these costs quantified and verified it is possible to assign to your products and services a price that will develop profitability without guessing!

Profitmover's know their costs!

P.S. The cost factors shown above are to be found on the following pages 45-76.

Failure to Understand Your Costs
in Relation to Your Pricing
is a Sure Way to Weak Profits
or Even Failure of Your Company

Chapter Eight

Are You Costing For Profit?

A primary objective of this book is to help you understand costs and cost relationships in your business environment. You may already keep a close eye on the costs of doing business by expanding your knowledge of the characteristics of your own market. But actually understanding costs and cost relationships is a process which involves quantifying the lines of business which contribute to your overall company objectives. This involves making certain key assumptions which will influence the financial conclusions you will form. The most important idea to remember is that financial analyses alone do not provide a true picture of your business for two reasons. First, there are other business considerations which must be given equal weight in your overall evaluation formula. Second, the financial reporting methods used in your business also greatly influence your results.

In this chapter we deal with other business factors which you will need to consider, including business mix, productivity, capacity, quality and allocations/financial analysis. Also, we will look at the financial reporting methods, specifically processes of allocation of costs and the carrying effects they can have on your bottom line.

The purpose of the following is to give you a sampling of the variables in your business analysis and to encourage your *investigation, testing and evaluation* of these various considerations in an effort to find the combination which best represents reality for your individual business.

Business Mix

There are many reasons that large corporations diversify into other lines of business. One of them is the decision to diversify to protect the profitability of another line of business. In other words, a company may choose to participate in a business which by itself, is marginally profitable, or perhaps even unprofitable, if the addition of that line of business enhances the overall financial position of the company. The same principle holds true in your business. As you complete the Cost/Analysis sections which follow, one or more of your lines of business may appear less attractive than the other.

The first and perhaps easiest conclusion to draw, if this is the case, is that more sales effort must be diverted from those lines to the more profitable lines of business. However, the consideration here is the effect of such a decision on the overall business picture. You must ask yourself, "Will this decision have an adverse effect on my other lines of business?" For example, a decision to shift sales emphasis away from one line of business could have a direct adverse impact on another line of business.

Considering these implications, the reaction might be different. In fact, the opposite reaction could be justified. You may decide that increasing sales efforts is an effective way of pumping more business into those lines of business which are more attractive. Thus, a healthy mix of business is very important, especially in an industry where the various lines of business feed each other due to their natural relationship. Always consider mix as a part of any financial analysis.

Productivity

Regardless of how favorably a financial analysis speaks for a line or piece of business, there is most always room for improvement. Increasing sales, increasing productivity and/or decreasing expense are three ways to achieve improvement.

Improving productivity is a process of measurement and reaction. It means defining current levels of production and investigating cost. Productivity is important in a service business which is labor intensive. Some productivity measures can be conveniently included at the bottom of a cost analysis worksheet in the form of ratios, percentages and guidelines. These provide your period-to-period benchmarks. You may also consider setting up some of your own productivity measures.

Capacity

A successful businessman once remarked that he loved to work on Saturdays and Sundays. When asked why anyone would want to spend his entire weekend at work, he reasoned this way, "Every penny I take in during the week goes right back out the door to pay my expenses. By the time Saturday comes, I've paid all my expenses, and every penny that comes in is PURE profit." This humorous response is not without merit. In fact, we all practice this every day. If you are in the trucking business, or if you are in the manufacturing business, you try to improve the output of your equipment to produce more units. By using the various capacities to their fullest, the less cost per unit, piece, or commodity. The new business term of 24/7 has taken its place in some industries when the facilities are used 24 hours a day, 7 days a week.

Putting all other considerations aside, there will be times when accepting a piece of business would not seem financially practical. However, if you have unused capacity in your system to handle the work, and the revenue will cover the costs associated with it, the revenue could be attractive. Not because it is profitable in and of itself, but because it lowers the cost base for the other revenues and makes them more profitable. Thus, volume increases, in the presence of capacity, are a good way to improve profitability by lowering unit costs.

The concept of capacity is especially important to understand due to the cyclical nature of a business. For example, in the slow winter months when your capacities are larger than in peak months, lowering the financial standards you have set for each piece of business may make sense. Your profits may be smaller in dollars because of the lower volume in business, but you may be able to maintain your profit margin as a percentage by doing so. In the summer months, as you approach a full capacity, raise your standards a bit by replacing a portion of your marginal business with more attractive business. Of course there will be accounts, which because of their volume, or the year-round nature of their business, must be protected. These should be protected to the greatest extent possible as the consequences of not doing so in the winter might be unfavorable.

Quality

We all know that customer satisfaction is our number one goal. Giving that satisfaction by doing a job right the first time is the least expensive way to reach that goal.

Failure to make sure that the proper documentation is completed by the salesperson can cause others to make mistakes. Failure on the part of operations personnel to properly perform can cause customer dissatisfaction and require additional labor to correct. Failure on the part of office personnel to document and bill customers in an orderly and timely fashion can cause complaints from the customer. All of these examples and others can cause additional cost to a company if quality isn't watched carefully. As Ford Motor Company says, "Quality is job one," and for management not to work diligently and consistently to improve quality of service will cause costs to climb, make the company uncompetitive, and lose customers.

Financial Analysis

Financial analyses can be a wonderful new tool for managing your business for profit. The main point to make in this discussion is that financial analysis must be truly reflective of your business to be of value. To obtain the ultimate benefit from the pages that follow, you should closely examine both your accounting methods and the allocation method which you use. Your objective should be to use systems that are consistent, adaptable and which represent your business. Remember, you know your business best.

Be a *Profitmover* and take time to complete a business analysis of your company.

*Allocations and Cost Accounting
are Required for Proper Distribution
of Revenues and Expenses!*

Chapter Nine

Do You Know Your Allocations
And Cost Accounting?

Cost accounting and cost allocation are to accountants as the "chicken and the egg" issue is to philosophers. There are many methods, most of which can be adequately defended. The method you choose must best state your costs within the parameters of your own accounting system. We will look at four such allocation methods, their characteristics, advantages and disadvantages.

The two cost categories we will discuss are "Direct" and "Indirect." Within each of these categories are variable and fixed costs which are defined as follows:

Direct Costs - Those which are a direct result of the performance of a business activity.

Indirect/Overhead Costs - Those which are incurred for the common benefit of all business activities.

Variable Costs - Those which fluctuate in proportion to the quantity of service rendered.

Allocation - The process of assigning costs to the functional line of business which caused them to happen.

A word of caution: If you do not fully understand the methods listed below be sure to get advice from your accountant.

With that introduction, let's look at the various methods of cost allocation you might choose to use. We will use the same sample throughout these examples so that you can see the resulting differences in each. These are fictitious numbers and will not resemble yours.

The Gross Margin Approach

This approach will differ from the others in that the only attempt here is to allocate direct costs, ignoring the indirect. Here the indirect expenses are treated as a separate line of business whose revenues equal the sum of the gross margins for the other lines of business.

	Revenue 1	Revenue 2	Revenue 3	Revenue 4	Revenue 5	Revenue 6	TOTALS	
REV.	100,000	80,000	150,000	230,000	75,000	75,000	710,000	
EXP.	60,000	50,000	100,000	170,000	55,000	40,000	475,000	*INDIRECT*
(+/-)	40,000	30,000	50,000	60,000	20,000	35,000	235,000	**165,000**

In this example all direct costs have been allocated. The gross margin is the difference between revenue and direct expense for each line of business. Although there is still $165,000 of indirect costs remaining, the total of the gross margins ($235,000) exceeds the cost. The profit for this company would be total gross margin less indirect expense, which equals $70,000. Since indirect costs are incurred for the common benefit of all business lines, no attempt is made to further allocate.

This method has two advantages; it precludes erroneous assumptions that are often made when allocating and may lead to false conclusions, and second it allows concentration on the control of direct and indirect costs, separately, by keeping them in separate pools. If costs are a problem, this can be a more precise method of tracking progress in theses areas.

The biggest disadvantage of this method is that it doesn't individualize profits for each line of business because it doesn't attempt full allocation. It does remain an attractive alternative if your concern is with the profitability of your business as a whole rather than of each individual line of business and/or the separate monitoring of direct and indirect costs.

Percent-of-Revenue Method

The first step here is the same as the previous example. Make as much direct allocation as your accounting method will allow. The percentage line shows the percent of total revenue represented by the revenue for each of the lines of business. This resulting percentage times the total of indirect expense would then equal the amount allocated to that line of business. Subtracting the allocated amount from the gross margin equals gross profit.

This approach makes one critical assumption—that there exists a direct relationship between revenue and overhead. In other words, each dollar that comes in causes a similar proportion of indirect expense to be incurred. Similarly, this method also relies on the assumption that the average price for each of the lines of business is approximately the same. For this to be true, the average revenue would need to produce about the same revenue as the average expense. If this is not the case, the allocation will provide a somewhat distorted picture.

	Revenue 1	Revenue 2	Revenue 3	Revenue 4	Revenue 5	Revenue 6	TOTALS	
REV.	100,000	80,000	150,000	230,000	75,000	75,000	710,000	
EXP.	60,000	50,000	100,000	170,000	55,000	40,000	475,000	*INDIRECT*
(+/-)	40,000	30,000	50,000	60,000	20,000	35,000	235,000	**165,000**

PCT.	14%	11%	21%	32%	11%	11%	100%

ALLOC.	23,239	18,592	24,859	53,451	17,430	17,430	**165,000**
GROSS PROFIT	16,761	11,408	15,141	6,549	2,570	17,570	

This distortion is evident in the examples since Revenue 4 has absorbed the majority of the indirect expense. This would not likely be the case as revenues might justify a smaller indirect expense allocation since some control is relinquished to another company. This method is good where accounting practices cannot facilitate another method, or where unitized revenues among the lines of business are approximately the same. The biggest disadvantage is the one we have shown above.

Percent-of-Other-Cost Method

This method is very similar to the Percent-of-Revenue method discussed above. Here the percentage line is the percent of total expense represented by the expense for the individual lines of business. The allocation (ALLOC) is the resulting percentage times the indirect expense pool. Again, the gross margin minus the allocated amount equals the gross profit.

The assumption here is that the proportion of expense to revenue is approximately the same. Other than this, little other cost is incurred. This method, however, makes a significant allocation of indirect expense to Revenue 4 since it has the highest revenue generated.

	Revenue 1	Revenue 2	Revenue 3	Revenue 4	Revenue 5	Revenue 6	**TOTALS**	
REV.	100,000	80,000	150,000	230,000	75,000	75,000	710,000	
EXP.	60,000	50,000	100,000	170,000	55,000	40,000	475,000	*INDIRECT*
(+/-)	40,000	30,000	50,000	60,000	20,000	35,000	235,000	**165,000**

PCT.	14%	11%	21%	32%	11%	11%	100%

ALLOC.	23,239	18,592	24,859	53,451	17,430	17,430	**165,000**
GROSS PROFIT	16,761	11,408	15,141	6,549	2,570	17,570	

Full Allocation of Costs

Although the accounting records of most companies are probably not detailed enough to effectively use this method, it remains the best and most accurate. Full Allocation of Costs is the process of changing indirect costs into direct costs. This can be done through a scientific set of tested assumptions or simply by managerial instinct. Of course the more scientific the approach, the more reliable the results.

Here we look at the component costs that comprise the pool of indirect costs in as much detail as possible. Our objective is to determine to what extent a functional line of business causes the incurrence of that indirect cost. For example, let's say that in my $165,000 pool of indirect costs, I have $100,000 in salary expense. If I can determine where the people included in that cost spend their time, I can divide their cost among the lines of business they serve. I can make that determination, as we said, by performing a time and motion study, by simply making an "educated guess," or something in between. This process can be applied to several of the items in your pool of indirect costs. You may find it feasible to allocate such expenses as salaries, wages, fringes, payroll taxes and many of the other items you will see in the Chart of Accounts to follow. Commissions and salaries are more likely to represent the preponderance of your indirect pool. These can be among the easiest costs to put through this allocation process.

It is unlikely that you will ever be able to make a truly full allocation. There will come a point where further allocation forces too many abstract assumptions. It is important that you recognize this point and not try to destroy the benefits you have created through logical allocation, with unreasonable assumptions.

At this point, choose the allocation method from those presented here, or any other which can be tailored to your system. Although the allocation of those remaining indirect costs is important, the impact of one method over another is much less since it is allocating a much smaller amount of dollars.

Conclusion

Financial analyses, such as those that will be presented throughout the remainder of this book, can be a wonderful new tool for managing your business for profit. The point in this discussion is that financial analysis must be truly reflective of your business to be of value. To obtain the ultimate benefit from the pages that follow, you should closely examine both your accounting methods and the allocation method which you use. Your objective should be to use systems that are consistent, adaptable and which represent your business. Remember, you know your business best.

Profitmover's know how to allocate and cost account!

*"Some of Us will Do Our Jobs Well
And Some Will Not,
But We will All Be Judged by Only One Thing —
The Result."*

— *Vince Lombardi*

Chapter Ten

Do You Know Your Cost Of Sales?

The obvious question the manager of any business should ask is, "What should I be paying my salespeople to develop and sell our products and services?" When we ask ourselves this question, we automatically know we need the right answers, but, in most cases managers and sales managers are just guessing and hoping they are right. That is why it is important for management and salespeople to understand the cost of sales principle.

Simply stated, cost of sales is the percent of cost, (i.e. salary, commissions, taxes and fringe benefits) of actual revenues sold. This can be accomplished by using a Cost of Sales Analysis.

Why Cost Of Sales?

Developing a system of measuring your sales department is extremely important for the following reasons:
1) It provides the opportunity to measure past sales results against future sales results.
2) It gives you timely measurements to compare against actual results.
3) It allows you to measure not only the company results, but each individual salesperson's results.
4) It helps establish realistic sales goals for the company and for the individual salesperson.
5) It helps to control sales costs.

There are two basic data bases used in evaluating your sales costs:
1) Gross Sales
2) Retained Revenue

Measurements

    Gross sales are all revenues received, including revenues that may be paid to others.

    Retained revenues are all revenues that are solely for the discretionary use of your company. In other words, monies that your company can use to pay its bills.

    The example of salesperson A.B. Smith, on pages 47 and 48 shows two ways a salesperson can be measured, both on a gross sales and retained revenue basis. As you can see, all of the actual costs Mr. Smith had in January are shown on lines 1-11. These figures show a percentage of costs to gross sales of 9.5 percent and cost to a retained revenue basis of 19.9 percent..

    I personally like sales goals established on retained revenue as it helps focus on the company's actual revenues. It also is easier for the salesperson to focus on developing a profitable order.

    A mix of sales can play a big part in the percentage of sales costs to gross sale and retained revenue. This is caused by certain sales having stronger gross margins than others. When establishing goals, it is important to look at and understand the mix of business each salesperson is selling.

SALESPERSON   *A.B. SMITH*   COMPANY <u>XYZ INC.</u>
Gross Sales   <u> X </u>   YEAR <u>   </u>
Retained Revenue <u>   </u>

COST OF SALES ANALYSIS

_____ Projected or _____ Actual Sales	$	**500,000**
Monthly Average	$	**41,667**
Acceptable Cost of Sales (10%	$	**50,000**
1. Commission/Salary	$	**38,000**
2. FICA	$	**2,250**
3. FUT	$	**187**
4. SUT	$	**375**
5. Worker's Comp	$	**413**
6. Medical & Dental	$	**1,500**
7. Sales Expense	$	**450**
8. Life Insurance	$	**200**
9. Pension/401K	$	**1,250**
10. Car	$	**3,017**
11. Other	$	
	$	
	$	

TOTAL	$	**47,642**

Expenses (Items 2-11)	$ **9,642**	(**1.9 %**)
Commission/Salary (Item 1)	$ **38,000**	(**7.6 %**)

TOTAL
    (Cost of Sales of
    all Items 1-11) $ **47,642**   (**9.5%**)

SALESPERSON   <u>A.B. SMITH</u>   COMPANY <u>XYZ INC.</u>
Gross Sales <u>   </u>   YEAR <u>   </u>
Retained Revenue   <u> X </u>

COST OF SALES ANALYSIS

_____ Projected or _____ Actual Sales	$	**240,000**
Monthly Average	$	**20,000**
Acceptable Cost of Sales (10%	$	**48,000**
1. Commission/Salary	$	**38,000**
2. FICA	$	**2,250**
3. FUT	$	187
4. SUT	$	375
5. Worker's Comp	$	413
6. Medical & Dental	$	**1,500**
7. Sales Expense	$	450
8. Life Insurance	$	200
9. Pension/401K	$	**1,250**
10. Car	$	**3,017**
11. Other	$	
	$	
	$	

TOTAL .... $ <u>**47,642**</u>

Expenses (Items 2-11) $ <u>**9,642**</u> (**4.1%**)
Commission/Salary (Item 1) $ <u>**38,000**</u> (**15.8 %**)

TOTAL
    (Cost of Sales of
    all Items 1-11) $ <u>**47,642**</u> (**19.9%**)

Understanding and Controlling
Overhead Costs (Fixed Costs)
Will Lead to Better Profits!

Chapter Eleven

Do You Know Your Overhead Costs?

The purpose of this chapter is to establish, annually, a method of accumulating overhead cost, which can be applied to various cost analyses in your various revenue lines.

The accounts shown on the following pages are those costs that normally fall under the heading of overhead or fixed cost. Generally speaking, overhead costs can be defined as those company-incurred costs that cannot be traced to a particular revenue producing function. In other words, overhead costs are indirectly incurred for the common benefit of all functions.

Once you have established your list of overhead accounts I suggest that you manage and control these fixed costs on a zero base budget process. Once you have established the total annual cost, don't exceed that figure! Every effort should be made to lower it, and by doing so your company will more than likely show a bigger profit.

Your accountant or CPA can help you establish a list of overhead accounts each year, so you will be able to apply this portion of expenses equitably to each area by using one of the options under the Allocations and Cost Accounting chapter previously discussed.

Once you know and understand your overhead costs, you will be able to better control and reduce them.

Profitmover's know their overhead cost!

COMPANY _____ DATE _____

OVERHEAD ACCOUNTS

ACCOUNT NAME	ACCOUNT NUMBER	
SALARIES:	**4100**	
Supervisory and Administrative Personnel	4100	$ _____
Clerical	4120	_____
Sales Salaries-Employees	4140	_____
Officers	4170	_____
Department and Division Managers	4190	_____
OTHER WAGES:	**4900**	$ _____
FRINGE BENEFITS:	**5000**	
Contributions to Union Welfare Funds	5010	$ _____
Employees' Group Insurance	5020	_____
Worker's Compensation	5030	_____
Pension and Retirement Plans	5040	_____
Vacation Pay	5050	_____
Holiday Pay	5060	_____
Misc. Paid Time Off	5070	_____
Other Employee Benefits	5090	_____
PAYROLL TAXES:	**5100**	
FICA Taxes	5110	$ _____
Federal Unemployment Taxes	5120	_____
State Unemployment Taxes	5130	_____
REPAIR MATERIALS (Other Than Vehicle):	**6500**	$ _____
Repair Materials-Building	6510	_____
Repair Materials-Equipment	6520	_____
Repair Materials-Furniture and Fixtures	6530	_____

ACCOUNT NAME	ACCOUNT NUMBER	
PRINTING AND OFFICE SUPPLIES:	**6600**	
Printed Forms and Office Supplies	6610	$ _____
Tariffs and Schedules	6620	_____
MISCELLANEOUS SUPPLIES	**6800**	$ _____
OUTSIDE SERVICES-REPAIRS:	**7200**	
(Other Than Vehicle)		
Outside Services-Building Repairs	7210	$ _____
Outside Services-Equipment Repairs	7220	_____
Outside Services-Furniture and Fixture Repairs	7230	_____
OTHER OUTSIDE SERVICES:	**7300**	
Janitorial Services	7310	$ _____
Watch and Alarm Services	7320	_____
Professional Services	7330	
UTILITIES	**7400**	$ _____
COMMUNICATIONS SERVICES	**7500**	$ _____
GENERAL EXPENSES:	**7900**	
Periodicals	7910	$ _____
Membership and Dues	7920	_____
Conventions and Meetings	7930	_____
Postage	7940	_____
Miscellaneous Corporate Expenses	7990	
DEPRECIATION:	**8100**	
Depreciation-Building and Structures	8140	$ _____
Depreciation-Furniture and Office Equipment	8150	_____
Depreciation-Undistributed Property	8170	_____
Depreciation-Miscellaneous Equipment	8190	_____

ACCOUNT NAME	ACCOUNT NUMBER	
AMORTIZATION EXPENSES:	**8200**	
Amortization of Leasehold Improvements	8210	$ _____
Amortization Expense- Other	8220	_____
RENT-OTHER THAN REVENUE EQUIPMENT:	**8300**	
Rent on Building Property	8310	$ _____
Rent on Office Equipment	8320	_____
Rent on Miscellaneous Equipment	8330	_____
TAXES AND LICENSES:	**8400**	
Real Estate and Personal Property Taxes	8410	$ _____
Other Taxes-Federal	8480	_____
Other Taxes-State and Local	8490	_____
INSURANCE:	**8600**	
Insurance on Buildings and Structures	8660	$ _____
Other Insurance Expenses	8690	_____
UNCOLLECTIBLE REVENUE	**8800**	$ _____
GAINS OR LOSSES ON DISPOSITION OF OPERATING ASSETS:	**8900**	$ _____
Gains on Disposition of Operating Assets	8910	$ _____
Losses on Disposition of Operating Assets	8920	_____
	TOTAL	$ _____

The Fruit of Our Labor is Manifested
by Understanding
its Cost and Productivity!

Chapter Twelve

Do You Know Your Labor Costs?

Labor is one of the BIGGEST cost areas in most companies. This requires management not only to understand the total loaded cost of an employee in a certain position, but also understand what the productivity standard should be.

To understand the total costs of an employee you need to develop a method that can give you the duty hour rate as shown in the format on the next page.

Regarding the method of calculation on the Duty Hour/Labor worksheet, the total possible annual work hours of 2,080 is an accepted standard, and the vacation time is an average of two weeks, as well as the average number of holidays being shown as seven.

A 10 percent non-productive hour calculation is used for those hours that cannot be billed. This non-productive time accounts for any labor functions that do not produce revenue for the company or for any activity for which you cannot charge. Each company should use its individual labor costs and fringe benefits when calculating the various "Duty Hour/Labor Rate", which will allow you to understand what your labor cost should be as a percent of revenue. What you need to ask yourself is "What should the percentage be in my company?" Once you know this percentage, you will be able to manage your labor cost so a better profit is realized.

Profitmover's control labor cost!

DUTY HOUR LABOR RATE WORKSHEET

	WORKER 1	WORKER 2	WORKER 3	WORKER 4	WORKER 5
Wages ($10.50 hr. X 2,080 hrs.	$21,840				
($10.00 hr. X 2,080 hrs.		$20,800			
($9.50 hr. X 2,080 hrs.			$19,760		
($7.50 hr. X 2,080 hrs.				$15,600	
($6.50 hr. X 2,080 hrs.					$13,520
($ hr. X 2,080 hrs.					
FICA (6.7 %)	1,463	1,394	1,394	1,045	906
Federal Unemployment (.8 % first $ 7,000)	56	56	56	56	56
State Unemployment (2.9 % first $ 12,000)	348	348	348	348	348
Pension ($ 181.65 mo. X 12)	2,180	2,180	2,180	2,180	2,180
Medical & Dental ($ 176.62 mo. X 12	2,119	2,119	2,119	2,119	2,119
Workers Compensation (Gross X .07840)	1,712	1,631	1,549	1,223	1,060
Other Taxes .6%	131	125	119	94	81
Total Annual Cost	29,849	28,653	27,455	22,665	15,971
Cost Per Production Hr. (1677 hr.)	$ 17.79	$ 17.06	$ 16.37	$ 13.52	$ 9.52

Production Hours:

Total Hours	2,080
Vacation Hours	- 80
7 Holidays	- 56
Breaks	- 81 (20 minutes -243 days)
Total Hours	1,863
Non-Productive Hrs. - 10%	- 186 *
TOTAL Productive Hours	1,677

* Unproductive time that cannot be billed for, i.e., lost time

Note: When developing an overtime rate from the above figures, be sure an effort is made to add only the taxes and benefits that are appropriate when paying overtime.

Controlling Inventory
Requires
Study and Restraints!

Chapter Thirteen

Are You Controlling Supplies & Material Cost?

Many of the companies I have worked with do not spend the necessary time controlling the costs related to purchasing supplies and materials. They do not understand the true cost of materials and supplies and they don't watch and control their inventories.

A recent statistical study showed that the cost of maintaining goods and materials in inventory averages about 2% per month. This covers financing, insurance, storage space/warehousing, inventory control and personnel to care for it. If you carry any stock for a full year its value is reduced by 24%. This can become very costly and reduce your ability to generate profits. I can assure you that major corporations like Ford, GM and IBM spend time and management making sure that purchasing, controlling inventory and costs are in line with certain benchmarks established for pricing a product or service at a reasonable profit.

Let's look at the areas that require your involvement so overall costs are kept as low as possible.

Purchasing
1. Develop a system (i.e. purchase order system) that requires the person requesting the materials or product to explain why he or she needs these items.
2. Do you need this quantity?
3. When do you need this product or materials and when do you plan on selling it?
4. Get more than one quote.
5. Does the provider offer time payment terms?
6. Check other company operations to see if they have any materials or product available.

Understand Costs
1. Compare cost with previous purchases.
2. Does the cost come within the parameters of the established pricing?
3. Ask for price reductions on large orders.

4. Send letter to all vendors indicating that you will not pay their invoice without securing a valid purchase order number.
5. Use just-in-time ordering process.
6. Monitor and watch shipping cost.
7. Direct-ship or drop-ship whenever possible.

Warehousing & Inventory Control

1. Develop and use a system (hopefully computer assisted) that can tell you what is in stock.
2. Maximize the space used for warehousing by racking and narrow aisle stacking.
3. Control amount of inventory by projected orders with the goal of turning both raw inventory and manufacture inventory every 30 to 60 days.
4. Dispose of slow moving or old inventory.
5. Use a sample material cost worksheet which can be found on page 63.

When you control the purchasing of supplies and materials as indicated above you will help your company make a better profit.

Profitmover's control purchasing and inventory!

DATE _____

MATERIALS COST WORKSHEET

CUSTOMER _____ ORDER # _____ JOB # _____

WORKERS_____

Quantity	Description	Unit Price	Net Amount

Shipping & Handling $ _____

Tax $ _____

TOTAL $ _____

Zero Defect is What Produces
Good Customer Relationships
and Better Profits.

Chapter Fourteen

Do You Understand Risk Costs?

Most companies spend very little time finding out or studying what their exposure is and what it costs to cover their liabilities. They call an insurance agent, get bids, and go with the lowest. Not very scientific. They leave it up to the insurance underwriter to tell them if the costs of claims are too high when they renew their insurance next time around. This should be known before someone on the outside tells the company.

I believe a company should keep track of its claims in such a way that it will know when it is starting to have a problem before the insurance company raises rates or cancels.

I recommend that a company appoint someone to keep track of claims by type and category using the Claims Analysis Worksheet found on page 67. By accumulating the claims information shown on the following pages, you can develop the data necessary for figuring the average claim cost that should be assessed for each transaction or line of revenue in your company.

The average hauling claim cost can be calculated by adding up the total claims for a given period and dividing by the total number of orders or units in the same period. Be sure that you use the total number of orders or units handled, regardless of whether there is a claim or not, or you will get a distorted claim cost per order.

Examples: (In the examples that follow, trucking industry orders are used to illustrate claims costs).

Revenue 1
> Time: <u>Jan. 1 - June 30</u>
> Number of Orders Manufactured: <u>83</u>
> Total Claims Paid by Company: <u>$1,684</u>
> Total Claims $1,684 ÷ # of shipments 83 = <u>$20.29</u> average

The above calculation indicates that a total of 83 orders were handled and claims costs paid by the company were $1,684, or an average claim cost of $20.29.

Revenue 2
    Time: <u>Jan. 1 - June 30</u>
    Number of Shipments Packed: <u>64</u>
    Total Claims Paid by Company: <u>$1,453</u>
    Total Claims $1,453 ÷ # of pack jobs 64 = <u>$22.70</u> average

The above calculations indicates that a total of 64 shipments were packed and claims costs paid by the company were $1,453, or an average claim of $22.70.

Revenue 3 - Hauling
    Time: <u>Jan. 1 - June 30</u>
    Number of Shipments Hauled: <u>110</u>
    Total Claims Paid by Company: <u>$4,382</u>
    Total Claims <u>$4,382</u> ÷ # of shipments hauled 110 = <u>$39.84</u> average

The above calculation indicates that a total of 110 shipments were shipped or hauled and claims costs paid by the company were $4,382 or an average claim of $39.84

When you start accumulating claims cost information it will help you understand what needs to be worked on, who the employee is that is causing the claim, what training is required, and what changes are required for safer working conditions. When you control and manage claims, you not only reduce costs, but improve customer service by reducing complaints. When this happens it is easier to make a profit.

Profitmover's work for zero defect!

Date _____

CLAIMS ANALYSIS WORKSHEET

TYPE OF CLAIM _____

	Order #	Date	Customer	$ Amount	$ Paid By Insurance	$ Paid By Company	Total	Remarks
1.								
2.								
3.								
4.								
5.								
6.								
7.								
8.								
9.								
10.								
11.								
12.								
13.								
14.								
15.								
16.								
17.								
18.								
	TOTAL							

Total $ claims paid by company $_____ ÷ total # order _____ =

$ _____ average claim cost per order.*

* Be sure the total number of orders handled in the period you are analyzing are included regardless of whether there is a claim or not.

Understanding and Controlling
Equipment Cost
Can Help Improve Profitability!

Chapter Fifteen

Do You Understand Your Equipment Costs?

Understanding and controlling equipment costs can also help improve profitability. It is also important to know what these costs are so your pricing is accurate, and when it is time to replace obsolete or non-productive equipment.

The information found on the following page can usually be extrapolated and collated from your books by your accountant either by type and groups of equipment, or by individual pieces of equipment.

Developing annual costs for a typical tractor/trailer unit, or any revenue-producing piece of equipment is accomplished by pulling fixed expenses from your books, and then figuring your variable expenses for each type of equipment by keeping track of actual fuel, tires, repairs and miscellaneous items, over a representative period of time of three to six months or a year. This data and information then becomes, by type of vehicle, representative of what the average cost would be per hour, per day and per mile, and then is used in developing the cost data in the analysis of hauling. See vehicle cost worksheet on page 70.

What you need to ask yourself is "What are my costs for running equipment and what should they be for our company to be price competitive?"

Profitmover's know and understand their equipment cost.

VEHICLE COST WORKSHEET

Type of Vehicle: *TRACTOR/TRAILER*	Company: XYZ		

Vehicle #: *841-29*		Date: *JAN.*	

Trailer #: *841-30*			

Costs:	Annual Expense	Costs Per Day	Costs Per Mile
FIXED EXPENSE:			
1. Depreciation	$4,452	$17.12	12.4c
2. Licenses & Permits	1,310	5.04	3.6
3. Interest	1,920	7.38	5.3
4. Van Equipment	800	3.08	2.2
5. Taxes	953	3.67	2.7
6. Insurance	5,200	20.00	14.5
7. **SUBTOTAL**	14,635	56.29	20.7
VARIABLE EXPENSES:			
8. Fuel & Oil	$8,676	$33.37	24.1
9. Tires	1,908	7.34	5.3
10. Repairs	4,392	16.89	12.2
11. Miscellaneous	252	.97	.7
(tolls, scales, etc.)			
12. **SUB-TOTAL**	15,228	58.57	42.3
13. TOTAL DIRECT COST: (LINE 7 + 12)	$29,863	$114.86	$83.0
FACTS:			
14. TOTAL ANNUAL MILES TRAVELED: 36,000			
15. TOTAL ANNUAL DAYS: 260			
16. PER HOUR COSTS:			

16. PER HOUR COSTS:

Annual cost $ 29,863   ÷   2,080   Hours = $ 14.36   per hour

Cost per day $ 114.86   ÷   8   Hours = $ 14.36   per hour

Space Requirements Can Be
The Largest Single Cost in a Company.

There is a Need to Control
and Utilize Space Efficiently
as it Can Have a Big Effect
on the Bottom Line.

Chapter Sixteen

Do You Understand And Know
Your Plant Or Warehouse Cost?

One of the most fascinating consulting jobs I have undertaken was for a company that packaged products for manufacturers and shipped them to customers. I was hired by the president who admitted candidly that though he couldn't prove it, he was certain that there was a bottleneck in the warehouse where packaged cartons were sent from the assembly department to be dispatched.

When I met the warehouse foreman who had his job for more than 15 years, I knew instinctively that he was the source of the problem. I was not yet aware how extensive the backlog of boxes was that sat for delayed shipment.

The man was tall and heavy-set with a round, jolly face and shrewd little brown eyes that crinkled jovially as he smiled. I soon discovered, that Frank was a petty tyrant, who considered the warehouse and shipping schedules his personal inviolate domain. He resented immediately my questions, my authority to ask them and to require him to follow my orders. But when the vice president who hired me gave him explicit instructions to do what I asked, he and his crew responded begrudgingly and slowly. As I had expected, what I had discovered was that no system existed to prioritize the daily movement of cartons according to shipping dates listed on manifests.

Worse, when I asked Frank where back orders were located and where cartons of products that had not been shipped were located, he shrugged and said, 'Oh don't worry about those things, I've got them all in my head."

When I pointed out to him that many of the cartons stored in the ready-to-ship area did not match the office lists, nor the inventory and should be in warehouse Number 7, he replied, "We move things around to make more room. Like I said, it's all in my head."

When I told him that he and his crew would have to sort out and move all the containers into the inventory warehouse where they were supposed to be, he almost blew his top.

He blinked and his face began to turn red. "We can't do that! It'll take a week at least! When I told him that order control depended upon accuracy, he shook his head. "Look, up in the office. They don't know what's going on. Some dame types up a list and they think they solved it all. It ain't that easy."

With the lack of systems displayed in the warehouse complex, it didn't take long to understand that *it wasn't easy at all*. It was a system of confusion run by a man who had been given no supervision or leadership. He had been left alone to create a gigantic bottleneck that was costing the company dearly. It was no wonder that it was losing business, fielding complaints from customers and regularly shipping finished containers late.

I recommended the plant foreman be replaced and a total and precise inventory be set up. The results in two months, with a reorganized warehouse team, was that all the storage sheds were resettled with cartons marked according to type and function of each container. A coherent and legible system of symbols was initiated so that cartons could be labeled according to shipping date priority.

The savings to the company, the president told me later, amounted to thousands of dollars. One of the largest single costs most companies have is space. It is either rented, leased or purchased. In my experience consulting with hundreds of companies, I find that management spends very little time understanding what the actual plant or warehouse costs are and how these expenses relate to the price of an item or service they are selling.

On page 76 I have included Plant/Warehouse Cost Analysis (a sample worksheet) that actually accumulates basic costs so you have a reliable method to amortize its cost into various prices you would or could charge a customer. Most managers just guess at these costs or assume they are picked up in the overhead allocation. When this happens the likelihood of having excellent profit margins is difficult.

Let's take a look in detail at the Plant/Warehouse Cost Analysis Worksheet on page 76 starting with **Section 1**.

Line A shows the total square footage of the building of 17,000 square feet, less 1,200 square feet for the office and 800 square feet for the packing and crating area, leaving a total of 15,000 square feet devoted to warehousing.

Line B shows the 15,000 square feet devoted to warehousing divided by the total square footage of the building of 17,000 = 88.23 percent, which is the percent of space devoted to warehousing. In the example shown on page 86, the dock, aisle and set-off space have been measured and determined to be 4,500 square feet, or 30 percent of 15,000. The 4,500 is then subtracted from the 15,000 square feet to arrive at the net square footage of 10,500 square feet available for rent.

Line C of 22 feet is the stack height available in the warehouse.

Line D of 231,000 cubic feet is obtained by multiplying line B, 10,500 square feet by the 22 feet of stack height.

Section II deals with the expense items found in a typical warehouse operation, the total annual cost by expense items, the percentage devoted to the warehousing function and the annual warehouse cost. An example of how this allocation works is shown in the line of rent/lease of $25,500 x 88.23 percent space devoted to actual warehousing = $22,498.65 that is devoted as true rent/lease expense charged to the warehouse function. Another example of this cost allocation is shown under the expense items of vaults and forklifts, which are allocated to the warehouse function at 100 percent..

As you can readily see in this section, the total building expenses of $49,800 are reduced to $44,939, the true allocation of expense that should be applied to the warehouse operations.

The next step under Section II is the application of overhead expense, and this is accomplished by multiplying $44,938.99 times the 35 percent overhead allocation = $15,728.65. This figure is then added to the $44,938.99 giving a total warehouse cost of $60,667.64. This allocation method is known as *percentage of other cost,* shown in Chapter 7.

Section III deals with the annual unit costs. Line A develops the annual cost per square foot of $5.78 by dividing the total warehouse cost of $60,667.64 by the total rentable square feet of 10,500.

Line B develops the annual cost per cubic foot of 26.2 cents by dividing the total warehouse costs of $60,668 by the total rentable cubic feet of 231,000. Line C develops the annual costs per vault/rack section of $164.41 by dividing the total warehouse costs of $60,668 by the total number of vaults/rack section 369 in the warehouse.

Section IV, Summary Cost Breakdown deals with developing the following:

per year ÷ 12 = per month ÷30 = per day

		per year	per month	per day
A.	Per square foot	5.78	.48	1.6¢
B.	Per cubic foot	26.2	2.2¢	.07
C.	Per vault/rack section	164.41	13.70	45.7¢

Keep in mind that the percentage of annual occupancy will also play a big part of how you price your space. You now know your cost at 100% occupancy and must set your prices accordingly considering your true annual occupancy percentage.

When you have completed this data cost sheet, you will be ready to start pricing your space at a profit.

Profitmover's know the cost of space so they can price the space at a profit!

PLANT AND WAREHOUSE COST ANALYSIS WORKSHEET

Date _1-1_   Warehouse   _#1_

I.   Warehouse Data

A. Total square footage of building **17,000**

    Less: Office Space................................ _1,200_

             Packing & crating...................... _800_ = ... **2,000**

B. Square footage devoted to warehousing **15,000**

    % of space devoted to warehousing

$$\frac{15,000}{B} \div \frac{17,000}{A} = 88.23\%$$

    Less docks, aisles & set-off space _30%_ = ... **4,500**

    Net square footage available for rent **10,500**

C. Stack height _22 FEET_

D. Net rentable cubic feet (BXC).. **231,000**

II: Costs:

Expense items	Total Annual Cost	x	%Devoted to Warehouse	=	Annual Warehouse Costs
Rent/Lease or Depreciation................	**$25,000**		**88.23%**		**$22,498.65**
Interest Expense					
Insurance	**3,900**		**88.23**		**3,440.97**
Maintenance	**1,500**		**88.23**		**1,323.45**
Utilities	**4,800**		**88.23**		**4,235.04**
Security	**600**		**88.23**		**529.38**
Taxes	**5,000**		**88.23**		**4,411.50**
Vault Depreciation or Rent	**4,000**		**100.00**		**4,000.00**
Forklift...	**4,000**		**100.00**		**4,000.00**
Others...	**500**		**100.00**		**500.00**
SUB-TOTAL	**49,800**				**44,938.99**
Overhead Allocation:Warehouse cost	**44,939 x 35%**			=	**15,728.65**
TOTAL WAREHOUSE COSTS..					**$60,667.64**

III.   Annual Unit Costs:

A. Cost per square foot

    Total warehouse costs **$60,668** ÷ Net rentable square feet _10,500_ = **$ 5.78**

B. Cost per cubic foot

    Total warehouse costs **$60,668** ÷ Net rentable cubic feet _231,000_ =   **26.2¢**

C, Cost per vault

    Total warehouse costs **$60,668** ÷ No. of vaults _369_   = **$ 164.41**

IV.   Summary Cost Breakdown:

	per year ÷ 12	=	per month ÷ 30 =	per day
A. Per square foot	**$5.78**		**.48**	**1.6¢**
B. Per cubic foot	**26.2¢**		**2.2¢**	**.07**
C. Per vault	**$164.41**		**$13.70**	**45.7¢**

NOTE: Section IV summary cost breakdown are based on occupancy of 100 percent

You Can't Measure
What You're Doing
Without Productivity Standards
and Benchmarks!

Chapter Seventeen

Have You Established Productivity Standards And Benchmarks For Every Employee In Your Company?

I'm amazed at the lack of communication concerning establishing productivity standards and benchmarks for employees. Most managers assume that their people know what standards or benchmarks are required of them to contribute to the profitability of the company. Not True! When I consult with a company, the first thing I ask of the manager is for him to describe the standards and benchmarks of production for each of his employees per job. Nine times out of ten the manager looks at me blankly and admits that no standards exist.

To demonstrate how important standards are to the bottom line, the response from employees in a workshop for a moving and storage company is revealing. They strongly expressed the desire to at least work towards obtaining industry productivity standards for the number of cartons they packed each day. This meant acknowledging how many pounds per hour they should load and unload, and what the density should be for loading a container. When I first asked about their productivity standards, they all looked at me a bit funny and finally one of the workers said, "We don't have any productivity standards and no one has ever talked to us about benchmarks".

Shame on management, I thought. After the workshop more than a half dozen workers came up to me while I was standing with the owner of the company and asked him, "Why haven't you told us about these standards before? We know we can attain or beat the industry standards, we just didn't know it was all that important".

Needless to say, the owner/manager was embarrassed and at a loss for words. I'm happy to report that the owner immediately took action and developed proper standards and benchmarks for his employees. As a result, in one year the productivity of the company's crews increased by more than 20%. Was this worthwhile? You bet it was, as it related directly to an increase of 3% points on the bottom line of the company or $320,000 in greater profit for the year.

One of the easiest ways to improve your bottom line is to improve productivity. When your employees don't know what is expected of them they have a tendency to do just enough to get by since they have no direction or goals to attain. When you sit down with them and explain what standards and benchmarks are required for their individual jobs to make the company profitable and if they beat these goals, they will earn more, the situation becomes a win-win one.

There is no question but that profits increase when employees have goals to meet. My strong recommendation is that you evaluate each hourly or salaried position in your company and establish standards and benchmarks for each. These goals should be shown in job descriptions and should be reviewed quarterly. Once you implement these standards, you will see a big change in your profits and you will start to be a ***Profitmover***.

Chapter Eighteen

Can You Pass The Company Analysis?

Before you read the next chapters, please complete the following questionnaire by circling yes or no. This company analysis, based on your answers, can provide you with an important picture of how your company stands. It is a valuable tool with which you can plot changes and chart progress. The example following of the critical value of the company analysis strikes home to many managers because it reveals a common lack of experience with financial and organizational issues that cost many companies profit losses.

I met Dick when he asked me to help him bring his moving and storage company around from a creeping loss position, like leaking water dribbling money away, to one of sound profit-making. The graduate of a business college, Dick was 35 years old, very aggressive and wanted to make a lot of money. He inherited the business from his dad who died of cancer and he was not really ready to take over. He was thrown into the job much faster than he should have been. That's when he called me and I sat down with him and gave him a road map to get his company moving in the right direction. He was the first one for whom I put together the company analysis.

Because of what he learned about his company from the analysis, it went from an operating ratio of 106 (which meant that he was losing six cents on every dollar or six dollars on every hundred dollars), to a profit of seven percent. Now he was making seven cents on every dollar he was bringing in — a complete turn-around for a company employing about 150 people with a monthly overhead of $800,000. The changeover in earnings was significant.

From the beginning, I advised Dick that he needed to know on a daily, weekly and monthly basis exactly how the company was operating and what his revenue stream was, so that changes could be made to reverse the loss situation. The first step was the Company Analysis. This gave Dick an accurate picture of where his company stood. The glaring inefficiencies were easy to spot so action could be taken.

COMPANY ANALYSIS

Financial Points

1. Collection agencies have filed or threatened to file lawsuits against our firm.   Y   N   ____

2. Tax liens have been filed against our firm.   Y   N   ____

3. We never use the "float" in our checking account in order to solve cash flow problems.   Y   N   ____

4. Our controller/bookkeeper does not spend any appreciable time (i.e. more than 2 hours/week) talking to vendors who are requesting payments.   Y   N   ____

5. We are "current" in all our withholding taxes and sales taxes.   Y   N   ____

6. The average collection period for our accounts receivable is no more than 40 days.   Y   N   ____

7. All of our accounts payable are being paid in a timely manner (30 days).   Y   N   ____

8. Financial statements consisting of at least an income statement, balance sheet, accounts receivable and accounts payable agings, are prepared monthly and reflect both the revenue and expenses for the period.   Y   N   ____

9. Inventory procedures are in effect which insure that we accurately know our useable inventory at the end of the month.   Y   N   ____

10. The accounts receivable balance appearing on our financial statement accurately reflects what our customers acknowledge they owe and what they are capable of paying under the terms of our agreements with them.   Y   N   ____

11. Our "cash in the bank" account balance accurately reflects the actual funds in the bank after all the checks have been written and mailed.   Y   N   ____

12. The accounts payable balance reflected in our financial statement includes all invoices that have been presented to us or payment, including those which we may be disputing.   Y   N   ____

Growth and Profitability

13. Unit sales volumes (numbers of units/hour/tons of merchandise or services billed) is decreasing.   Y   N   ____

14. The company has reported a pretax profit (excluding extraordinary items) for the preceding two years and expects to report a profit this year.   Y   N   ____

15. Selling, general and administrative expenses as a percent of sales are increasing.   Y   N   ____

16. The gross profit margin for our major core products has increased over last year's profit margin.   Y   N   ____

17. Major decisions about new business, new products, new markets and/or acquisitions reflect a clear organizational strategy.   Y   N   ____

18. The turnover rate of our inventory (number of turns/year) has improved over last year's results.   Y   N   ____

Control Systems

19. The company has a business plan that sets forth the company's strategic and operational objectives and programs for the ensuing year.   Y   N   ____

20. The company operates in accordance with a budget and cash management system that is consistent with its objectives; expenditures against the budget are recorded and monitored; and substantial deviations are periodically analyzed.   Y   N   ____

21. The company's sales organization prepares sales forecasts and its performance against the forecast is monitored. These forecasts are used to establish inventory and/or personal levels of production.   Y   N   ____

22. The company has a program to quantitatively measure customer satisfaction   Y   N   ____

23. Individual responsibilities for monitoring and achieving financial goals are clearly defined.   Y   N   ____

Management

24. Our company has a well-defined mission and set of goals, which is frequently communicated to our employees. The mission and goals are in writing and a copy is available.   Y   N   ____

25. The chief executive officer frequently interacts with employees at various levels of the company.   Y   N   ____

26. Employees in our company are well informed as to how well or how poorly the company is meeting its stated objectives.   Y   N   ____

27. Our company lacks resources (money, equipment, space, personnel) to meet its short-range objectives and fulfill its contractual obligations.   Y   N   ____

28. Major decisions such as organizational changes, capital appropriations and new facilities are guided by a formal, well-defined approval process.   Y   N   ____

29. A single individual has ultimate responsibility for the company's day-to-day operating decisions.   Y   N   ____

Key Managers

30. All of the managers who report to the CEO are qualified by education, experience, loyalty, motivation and competence.   Y   N   ____

31. The turnover in management staff has been greater than 20% per year.   Y   N   ____

32. There are employees in the organization who are being carried because of family relationships, longevity of service, emotional ties and other non-economic reasons.   Y   N   ____

33. The performance of the firm cannot be improved by replacing any of the key managers.   Y   N   ____

The Management/Board Relationship

34. The members of the board of directors are independent-minded and intelligent businessmen and women whose education and experience encompass the technical financial and marketing aspects of the industry in which the company operates.   Y   N   ____

35. There is a lack of mutual rapport, trust and respect between the chief executive and the members of the board of directors.   Y   N   ____

36. All of the directors come to the board meeting prepared to discuss the relevant issues and participate in a constructive manner.   Y   N   ____

37. The owners, or major stockholders who are active in management and the affairs of the firm work very well together; they communicate with each other and in groups, openly and frankly, and have mutual respect for each other's opinions.   Y   N   ____

38. The board of directors and/or management meetings are very productive, and the key issues affecting the health and growth of the company are presented with adequate analytical data and are thoroughly discussed. Rational, and timely decisions are usually made. Y   N   _____

OVER-Diversification, OVER-Leverage, and OVER-Expansion

39. The key managers of the company are able to carry out their responsibilities within the normal work week and rarely have to work evenings or weekends. Y   N   _____

40. The key functions of the company are adequately staffed with individuals who have the capability to handle their responsibilities in the normal day-to-day manner. Y   N   _____

41. The ratio of the company's total debt to equity increased over the last year. Y   N   _____

42. Debt service (interest plus principle) as a percent of gross profit, has increased over last year's figure. Y   N   _____

Banking Relationships

43. We frequently receive calls from our bank, advising us that our account is overdrawn. Y   N   _____

44. We are current in all of our interest payments to our bank and conform with all of the provisions of our loan agreement. Y   N   _____

45. Our banker is friendly, cordial and cooperative and is always eager to assist. Y   N   _____

46. Our banker calls frequently to inquire about the status of the loan and asks very piercing and serious questions. Y   N   _____

47. Our banker has inquired about our willingness to pledge additional collateral (company or personal) to secure our loans. Y   N   _____

Legal Affairs

48. Except for collection efforts being pursued against delinquent accounts receivable, the company is not involved in any litigation. Y   N   _____

49. Assuming the company is currently involved in litigation, as the defendant, and the "worst-case" scenario should occur, the company would be able to pay the resulting judgment and still comfortably finance its continuing operations. Y   N   _____

50. In the case where the company is involved in a lawsuit in which it is the plaintiff, the minimum expected recovery will exceed the maximum legal cost to be expended. Y N ____

51. The CEO of this company spends more than 10% of his time on the legal affairs of the corporation, including regulatory and litigation matters. Y N ____

Single Customer/Single Vendor Dependency

52. More than 35% of the company's receivables or inventory is associated with one customer. Y N ____

53. In the event the company should lose a major customer to a competitor, the company could be reorganized so that profitability would not be affected. Y N ____

54. In the event the company's major customer filed bankruptcy, so that all the associated receivables and unique inventory had to be written off, the resulting write-down of assets would not jeopardize the requirements of the company's agreements with the bank. Y N ____

55. If any of the company's material or support service suppliers suddenly went out of business, the company could easily replace the supplier in a time frame that would not affect sales levels, contractual obligations or profitability. Y N ____

56. All of the company's existing suppliers are providing material and services on schedules and of the quality that are consistent with the company's obligations to its customers. Y N ____

57. The market for the company's major products and services is quite soft and we must cut prices frequently to preserve our market share. Y N ____

58. Our company is among the top four firms (in terms of market share) for the major markets that we serve. Y N ____

59. Our pricing policy is tied to the dominant firm in our industry and our price increases and decreases frequently follow their lead. Y N ____

60. We have, in the ordinary course of business, been able to replace products that competition and technology have made obsolete. Y N ____

TOTAL ____

Calculating the Index

To find your score, compare your answers to those listed in the scoring key. When your answer agrees with the key shown on page 89, give yourself the indicated number of points.

Add up your points and compare the total to the levels listed below to determine your business health.

0 to 20 Points: You Passed the Physical
Your business is probably in top condition. If you scored in this range, your company appears to be operating smoothly.

Prescription: Look over the answers that contributed points to your score and discuss those areas with your management staff. Investigate what corrective measures are appropriate. Establish a priority list of items and work on that list diligently to keep your business in top form.

20 to 50 Points: Your Business Is Running a Fever
No need to panic, but if you scored in this range your company has some serious problems which must be addressed immediately. Your firm is vulnerable to any number of factors or events that could lead it into a downward spiral.

Prescription: Discuss the issues raised by the test with your management team and get its suggestions for corrective action. Consider getting outside help to formulate and implement solutions in those areas where you may not be able to take appropriate action yourself.

51 or more Points: Surgery Is Indicated
This is an emergency alert. If you scored in this range, your company is already in a tailspin and is a candidate for the bankruptcy court.

Prescription: Your high score indicates that your firm does not currently have the skills to stop the tailspin and formulate and implement a turnaround program. Call in a turn-around specialist immediately.

Scoring Key

Number	Answer	Points		Number	Answer	Points
1.	(Y)	3		31.	(Y)	2
2.	(Y)	3		32.	(Y)	2
3.	(N)	1		33.	(N)	1
4.	(N)	1		34.	(N)	2
5.	(N)	3		35.	(Y)	3
6.	(N)	2		36.	(N)	2
7.	(N)	3		37.	(N)	3
8.	(N)	2		38.	(N)	3
9.	(N)	2		39.	(N)	1
10.	(N)	3		40.	(N)	2
11.	(N)	3		41.	(Y)	2
12.	(N)	3		42.	(Y)	2
13.	(Y)	1		43.	(Y)	3
14.	(N)	1		44.	(N)	3
15.	(Y)	3		45.	(N)	2
16.	(N)	1		46.	(Y)	2
17.	(N)	2		47.	(Y)	3
18.	(N)	1		48.	(N)	1
19.	(N)	2		49.	(N)	3
20.	(N)	3		50.	(N)	2
21.	(N)	3		51.	(Y)	1
22.	(N)	2		52.	(Y)	3
23.	(N)	1		53.	(N)	3
24.	(N)	2		54.	(N)	3
25.	(N)	2		55.	(N)	3
26.	(N)	1		56.	(N)	1
27.	(Y)	3		57.	(Y)	3
28.	(N)	1		58.	(N)	1
29.	(N)	3		59.	(Y)	1
30.	(N)	1		60.	(N)	2

*Decisions Should Be Based
on the Core Values
of Your Financial Statements.*

Chapter Nineteen

Do You Understand And Know
What Big Questions To Ask
When Analyzing Your Financial Statement?

So what are the big questions? Let me explain. After consulting with various types of businesses, it became apparent to me that most managers who analyze monthly financial statements spend very little time studying the results. Invariably, they turn to the last page of the computer run and look for the profit line to see what they made or lost and that's it. I believe that managers need to review and study their financial statements in more detail to be able to determine the continuing health of their companies. Five basic questions should be asked when a statement is reviewed:

- Did we meet our revenue goals for the month?
- Are the direct costs as a percentage of revenue in line with our forecast?
- Did we meet our gross margin percentage?
- Are our fixed costs in line as forecasted?
- Did we meet our profit goals as a percent of revenue?

If after these questions have been asked, you are not satisfied with the results shown on the Financial Statement, then a study should be made of the financial aspect in question, whether it be sales/revenues, direct cost, gross margin, fixed costs or profit. A good way to keep track of this on a monthly basis and year-to-date is to use the monthly review and analysis report as shown on pages 92-95. Your company deserves and requires your time for a few hours each month in the studying of trends and results so change can be made to help attain the profits you are looking for.

You're not a *Profitmover* if you don't!

COMPANY_____

DATE _____

MONTHLY REVIEW AND ANALYSIS REPORT

I. FINANCIAL

	MONTH	YTD
1. BUDGETED REVENUE	_____	_____
ACTUAL REVENUE	_____	_____
DIFFERENCE	_____	_____

COMMENTS _____
_____
_____

	MONTH	YTD
2. BUDGETED OPERATING PROFIT	_____	_____
ACTUAL OPERATING PROFIT	_____	_____
DIFFERENCE	_____	_____

COMMENTS _____
_____
_____

	GOAL	ACTUAL
3. MONTHLY PERCENTAGE REVIEW		
REVENUE	_____ %	_____ %
COST OF SERVICES SOLD	_____ %	_____ %
GROSS MARGIN	_____ %	_____ %
OVERHEAD	_____ %	_____ %
OPERATING PROFIT	_____ %	_____ %
OTHER INCOME/EXPENSE	_____ %	_____ %
PRE-TAX PROFIT	_____ %	_____ %

COMMENTS _____
_____
_____

	GOAL	ACTUAL
YEAR-TO-DATE PERCENTAGE REVIEW		
REVENUE	_____ %	_____ %
COST OF SERVICES SOLD	_____ %	_____ %
GROSS MARGIN	_____ %	_____ %
OVERHEAD	_____ %	_____ %
OPERATING PROFIT	_____ %	_____ %
OTHER INCOME/EXPENSES	_____ %	_____ %
PRE-TAX PROFIT	_____ %	_____ %

COMMENTS _____
_____
_____

MONTHLY REVIEW AND ANALYSIS REPORT

4. P & L / BALANCE SHEET RATIO GOALS ANALYSIS

	LAST YEAR	CURRENT
CURRENT RATIO	_____	_____
QUICK RATIO	_____	_____
DEBT TO WORTH	_____	_____
SALES TO ASSETS	_____	_____
RETURN ON ASSETS	_____	_____
RETURN ON INVESTMENT	_____	_____
ACCT. PAYABLE TURNOVER	_____	_____
ACCT. RECEIVABLE TURNOVER	_____	_____
D.S.O.	_____	_____
BREAK-EVEN POINT	_____	_____

II. OPERATIONAL AND WAREHOUSE GOALS AND RATIO

1. CLAIMS & SAFETY

	GOAL	ACTUAL
SAFETY	_____	_____
HAULING CLAIMS (handling claims)	_____	_____
PACKING CLAIMS (handling claims)	_____	_____
WAREHOUSE CLAIMS	_____	_____
OVERALL CLAIMS	_____	_____
CLAIMS % TO TOTAL REVENUE	_____	_____

2. OPERATING LABOR COSTS

	BUDGETED	ACTUAL
REGULAR	_____	_____
OVERTIME	_____	_____
CONTRACT & TEMPS	_____	_____
TOTAL	_____	_____
MONTHLY LABOR %	_____	_____
YEAR-TO-DATE LABOR %	_____	_____
DEBIT BALANCE %		_____

MONTHLY REVIEW AND ANALYSIS REPORT

3. MAINTENANCE & REPAIR COSTS TO REVENUE

	MONTH	YTD
	_____	_____

4. REPAIRS % TO TOTAL REVENUE

	MONTH	YTD
	_____	_____

5. WAREHOUSE REVENUE TO SQUARE FEET RATIO

MONTHLY
_____ REV. ÷ _____ SQ. FT. = _____

YEAR-TO-DATE
_____ REV. ÷ _____ SQ. FT. = _____

6. STORAGE REVENUE TO RENT OR WAREHOUSE COST

	MONTH	YTD
	_____	_____

III. CUSTOMER SERVICE

1. NUMBER OF ORDERS AVAILABLE TO HANDLE THIS MONTH _____

2. AVG. # OF ORDERS HANDLED PER CUST. SERVICE PERSON _____

IV. SALES DEPARTMENT

	BUDGETED	ACTUAL
1. MONTHLY RETAINED SALES	_____	_____
2. YEAR-TO-DATE RETAINED SALES	_____	_____
3. COST OF SALES	_____	_____
4. CLOSING RATIO	_____	_____
5. TOTAL SALES DEBIT BALANCES	_____	_____
6. AVERAGE SALES DEBIT BALANCES	_____	_____
7. BOOKING	_____	_____

	MONTH	YTD
20_ _	_____	_____
20_ _	_____	_____
DIFFERENCE	_____	_____

8. MARKET SHARE AS OF _____(Date)

	TERRITORY TOTAL	COMPANY TOTAL
BRANCH A	_____	_____
BRANCH B	_____	_____
BRANCH C	_____	_____
BRANCH D	_____	_____
BRANCH E	_____	_____

V. ACCOUNTING DEPARTMENT

FINANCIALS COMPLETED BY 12TH   _____

DRIVERS' PAYMENTS COMPLETED WEEKLY?   _____

SALESPERSONS' PAYMENTS COMPLETED?   _____

FLASH REPORT COMPLETED DAILY?   _____

BALANCE SHEET ACCOUNTS RECONCILED?   _____

ANALYSIS ISSUED BY 15TH?   _____

BILLING TERM   _____

D.S.O.   _____

Credit Given Wisely and Controlled
Means Good Cash Flow.

Credit Given Without Thought or Control
Will Cause Poor Cash Flow.

Chapter Twenty

Are You Controlling Your Credit?

Credit control is a real bugaboo with a lot of companies and it is the process I am often called on to make effective. I can't go in with a crowbar to threaten the bookkeeper or the accountant to shape up or else. But what does work is to sit quietly and discuss the very reasonable necessity of setting up clear billing instructions with customers.

It is astonishing how many people in the credit department of companies hate to talk to customers about paying their bills. There seems to be a natural reluctancy, almost an embarrassment to tell the customer what the company's credit terms are. This is certainly true of salespeople.

I remember the accountant who said to me, "The boss is always after me to get the receivables collected in a timely fashion, but I just hate to talk about terms with customers."

I understand this attitude, but I have converted a lot of credit people by making a simple statement: Customers expect to pay for the products or services they have purchased. It is important for them to know the conditions for the payments they must make.

The most effective methods to help the customer pay his bills in a timely manner are three-fold:

1. Make your terms clear.
2. Present the options you offer for payment.
3. Thank your customer for the order.

Every company runs its business differently based on customer needs, type of business and competition. Most companies, I have discovered, spend very little time controlling credit and in some cases have no written credit policy at all. A good credit policy goes hand in hand with a good collection policy. If certain things are not controlled properly via a well-written credit policy, it can become very difficult to make collections on a timely basis, or collect at all.

I recommend adoption of the following Cardinal Rules and Credit Information flow as part of your credit policy:

- No salesperson can give credit approval without following the written company policy and procedure.
- All sales are COD unless proper credit approval is given per credit policy.
- All invoices are Due and Payable Upon Receipt.

- Any customer who wishes credit must fill out a Credit Application prior to credit being given. (A sample copy of a credit application can be found on page 99.)
- To insure customer credit worthiness, the company should use an outside credit rating service such as Dun & Bradstreet.
- When you write your credit policy be sure everyone understands who has the authority to grant credit.
- Hold training sessions with all salespeople and customer service personnel on the company credit policy. Make sure they understand the policy, how to sell and explain it to customers, and who has the authority to grant credit.
- Proper communications regarding credit is important. Someone, i.e., salesperson, must explain the terms and conditions of obtaining credit. (Must be in writing also)
- Your records must be set up to show each customer's status and payments quickly.
- Be prompt in invoicing. Late invoices encourage late payment.
- Your intelligence regarding customer's financial status is important. Scan financial and trade press reports.
- Be consistent regarding issuing credit. Try not to make special concessions to big customers

Profitmover's have a strong credit policy in effect which helps cash flow!

CREDIT APPLICATION

We, the undersigned, (hereinafter referred to as customer) hereby apply for credit for the payment of services provided by _____ (hereinafter referred to as provider). CUSTOMER promises to pay all bills rendered pursuant to credit given the PROVIDER in accordance with the terms provided herein.

Business Name: _____ Telephone:_____
Address:_____ City: _____ State: _____Zip: _____
Accounts Payable Contact _____ Extension _____ Fed ID#_____

PARTNERSHIP [ ] PROPRIETORSHIP [ ] INCORPORATED [ ] STATE OF INCORPORATION:

Proprietors, Partners or Officers:
Name: _____ Title:_____
Name: _____ Title:_____

TRADE REFERENCES:

Name: _____ Address: _____ City: _____ State:_____ Zip:_____
Name: _____ Address: _____ City: _____ State:_____ Zip:_____
Name: _____ Address: _____ City: _____ State:_____ Zip:_____

Bank Reference:_____ Address: _____
Account Number: _____ Contact: _____ Telephone: _____

SIGNATURE AND CUSTOMER AGREEMENT: Everything I have stated in this application for credit is correct to the best of my knowledge. PROVIDER is hereby given permission to check my credit references or other information on this application and to obtain a consumer credit report to check my credit standing. I understand that payment terms are NET 30 DAYS, that a finance charge of 1-1/2 percent per month will be charged on the unpaid balance of past due accounts, and that the account will be subject to termination should it become past due. In the event of any breach of contract and/or default by CUSTOMER, PROVIDER shall be entitled to any and all remedies available at law or in equity. Additionally, should said breach or defaulted account(s) be referred for collection, the undersigned CUSTOMER, in addition to the amount showing shall pay: a) the greater of the actual cost of collection or a minimum amount of THIRTY percent (30%) of the principal balance: and b) actual attorney's fees and costs, if any incurred. This agreement shall be governed by the laws of the State which is the corporate office of PROVIDER. In the event of a lawsuit or other legal proceeding, Customer covenants and agrees, at the PROVIDER'S option, that may be the proper venue and that the appropriate court of _____ retains both in remand in personam jurisdiction over CUSTOMER and over all of CUSTOMER'S assets.

CUSTOMER'S
SIGNATURE:_____ TITLE:_____

PRINT NAME: _____ DATE: _____

Develop a Sense of Urgency
in Collections
of Receivables.

Remember Cash Flow
is the Blood Line
for Success in a Company!

Chapter Twenty One

How Good Are You
At Collecting Your Receivables?

It is vital to your company health to train people to collect money owed in a firm, courteous manner. Your objectives must be to collect your accounts receivable so effectively that you need never to borrow money to supplement your cash flow.

Also, it is vital that the collectors in your company should be familiar with the collection standards in your industry.

One company I know is so effective training people to collect receivables that an incentive program is offered to employees with the best collection records, The manager I am referring to rewards good performance by giving Friday off, rather than a cash bonus to outstanding collectors. This has worked so well, that the employees rush to the post office to collect the mail to see if the checks have arrived.

If you are not good at collecting receivables, it is more than likely that you have a cash flow problem and need to borrow money from your bank to cover payroll and expenses. When this happens you're stealing profit dollars off your bottom line.

First some facts: The longer it takes you to collect a receivable, the less likely you will be paid. Based on historical averages of collections, the following will take place.

Dollars Past Due	Percent Recovered	Percent Loss
120 day	80%	20%
180 day	67%	33%
1 year	45%	55%
2 years	23%	77%

Collecting money due requires constant vigilance and good management to control past due accounts and collect in a timely manner. Between high pressure tactics that alienate customers and lenient policies that jeopardize cash flow lies the right way to do the job. Persistence and consistency is the real key to proper collection, but having a system in place that monitors accounts daily will help you spot potential collection problems.

What should your policy be regarding collecting your money? The answer is found in your credit policy. If it is *Due And Payable Upon Receipt* and you have not received a payment within 15 days of mailing, a phone call is required requesting payment now! If your policy is *Net 30 Days* and you haven't received payment in 35 days from the date of mailing, a phone call is required requesting payment. Now! Sending Past Due letters doesn't do it any more. Collection phone calls made persistently and consistently are your best bet for collecting money. Going directly to the creditor's place of business requesting a check can be effective.

Strong collection goals and personal responsibility should be established with measurement as follows:

    (a) Never allow your collections to exceed 10% of your total receivables over 60 days.

    (b) A day's sales outstanding (D.S.O.) goal of __X__ days should be put in place. (35 to 40 days or less).

    (c) Appoint someone to be responsible for collections and for meeting the standards and benchmarks set by management for collections.

    (d) When you have credit sales it is important to check average monthly receivables against annual credit sales. If the monthly receivables are $250,000 and your credit sales are $1,555,000 you have a turnover of 6.22. Whether that turnover is good or bad depends on your historical benchmark and what is considered as an industry standard.

The rule of thumb used today by most companies for payment of what they owe is "Don't pay the bill until they ask for it". In fact some companies don't pay you until you ask twice. It's the old cash flow game. In other words use someone else's money instead of borrowing from a bank to which you have to pay interest. When you allow someone else to keep your money, shame on you! When you let this happen you are taking dollars off the bottom line. Remember, if your profit margin is 10% you will need additional sales of $100,000 to make up a $10,000 accounts receivable loss. When you think about this it's a real eye opener and a no-brainer. Work hard at collecting your money on a timely basis.

Profitmover's collect on time what is rightfully theirs!

Chapter Twenty Two

Do You Work At Increasing Cash Flow?

One of the companies that hired me to help them increase their cash flow was a medium-size midwest-printer whose specialty was manufacturing books for publishers. Calling me in to advise them on how to improve their cash flow revealed several serious problems. When I learned about the debacle that was created by the company's recent failure to deliver a large order when it was promised, I realized that difficulties facing the printer went far deeper than cash flow.

The large order the company received from a West Coast publisher of health care books was for 125,000 copies of a book written by a physician. It was to be used in a promotion campaign by one of America's giant pharmaceutical companies directed to primary care physicians around the United States. Each physician was to receive a copy of the book, compliments of the pharmaceutical house.

The order to the publisher from the pharmaceutical company amounted to $1,375,000, or $11 a copy. In turn, the publisher agreed to pay the printer $ 262,000 for printing the books and delivering them in three truckloads to the warehouse of the pharmaceutical company. Since the order to the printer specified delivery dates, number of books in each shipment and freight to be paid, it was crucial that the printer met its contracted obligations on time. A down payment was made to the printer of $131,000.

From that point on, the printer deviated from the schedule and it became obvious to me why this happened. Convinced that it could slip short-run jobs in between the large print runs of the major order, the printer figured he could piggyback profits by fudging on the big order delivery dates and number of books shipped in each truckload. It was a short-sighted and disastrous decision of management that had serious consequences. The pharmaceutical house complained to the publisher that the late delivery of orders had forced them to reschedule their promotional campaign to the doctors. The publisher, furious at the printer because they were billed for excessive freight charges and because of the tardiness in delivery, threatened a law suit and never again placed an order with the printer.

The moral of this story is that if the printer had installed realistic cash flow management systems, credit and collection policies—as I advised management to do when I was called in belatedly—they would never have found themselves in a financial crunch which made it tempting to disappoint an important customer and create a fallout that drove many other valuable accounts away.

Accelerating receipts is one way to enhance cash flow, but it's not easy; customers are always trying to slow their own cash outflows. So start by improving your billing and collection procedures. Here are some ideas.

Billing Procedures

1. Reduce the time between shipping, invoicing, and second notices on billings. Also establish special procedures for expediting the billing of high-dollar invoices. Try to bill immediately (within one or two days after shipment). **Even better:** Anticipate large billings and bill on the date of shipment.
2. Cycle your accounts receivable billings so that the monthly statement is sent to the customer several days before the end of the month. This approach should result in quicker payment.
3. Establish minimum order and invoice amounts for credit sales. (**Example:** If your average order is $200, you may wish to charge a $10 service fee on orders under $50.)
4. Schedule due dates for payment based on when the **job or product was delivered**, rather than when the customer received the invoice.

Collection Procedures

1. Review credit and collection policies to determine factors that hinder cash flow, such as continued extension of credit to slow-paying or seriously delinquent customers.
   Advisory: Collection efforts are most effective when you establish **firm** policies, put them in writing, and apply them consistently. Keep in mind that even a one-time deviation in the enforcement of the company's standard policies may become a "new policy" in the eyes of the customer for whom you made the exception.
2. Settle disputes with customers **immediately**. Find out the exact nature of the problem and then take the necessary steps to remedy it. This is especially important with customers who insist that they're withholding payment because of a problem with the order.
3. Your first contact with late-paying customers should be a telephone call rather than a delinquency letter. This will quickly determine whether there is a problem. It also alerts customers to the close attention you pay to monitoring your accounts receivable.

4. Charge interest on delinquent accounts (1% to 1 1/2 % per month on outstanding balances). If a customer is really slow and the amount due is sizeable, try to get a formal note with a specific repayment schedule.

5. Consider providing your salespeople with an incentive to assist in collecting the past-due amount by withholding all or part of their commissions until the accounts receivable is paid. (Be aware, however, of the impact this might have on your marketing division and on future sales.)
   Advisory: Have your bookkeeper provide a list of slow payers to all sales-people. Advise them as to how much credit can be extended to these customers. They may decide to concentrate on better paying accounts, particularly if their commissions are affected.

6. Look into establishing a lockbox service with banks in cities strategically located around your distribution area, so that payments from large customers reach a lockbox in one day.

7. Set up a system for quickly identifying delinquent accounts, especially on new customers. Consider the possibility that some "new" customers may have brought their business to you because other suppliers refused to deal with them or cancelled their credit. Of course, check out all new customers before extend-ing any credit: get references, ie. D&B, and call the customer's bank. (Note: Your bank may be able to help you check out any new customers.)

8. If you're seriously worried about an account, indicate to the customer that on all future purchases, you will require cash in advance or on delivery. (This strat-egy may provoke them to clean up old balances and pay on time in the future.)
   Cost of collections: Your delinquent accounts probably range in size from very small to very large. The in-house fixed costs of collecting (telephone calls, letters) on each account is about the same, no matter how large the amount outstanding. So you will want to concentrate your collection efforts on the larger delinquent accounts. A collection agency, on the other hand, usually takes a percentage of the amount recovered (frequently one-third to one-half).

9. Many larger companies and government organizations traditionally are late payers. Consider this possibility when bidding for their business and be sure to find out what their payment procedures are before you quote prices on your products or services.

10. Be careful if you're selling to customers in foreign countries. Collecting a delin-quent international account can be very costly. Even getting a check to clear can take far longer than domestically. Also, don't forget about exchange rate

variations. Talk with your banker **before** engaging in foreign transactions for the first time.

Important: In order to protect against exchange rate changes, consider hedging or requiring that the amount be paid in U.S. dollars.

Ways To Decrease Cash Outflow

Delaying disbursements to the latest possible date, while taking advantage of significant discounts and being careful not to jeopardize supplier relations, is a prime objective of cash flow management.

Consider these ideas.

1. Establish a system that provides for the payment of large, **non-discount** bills at the latest date possible.
    Example of savings: If you delay a $20,000 bill by 30 days, at a 10% interest rate, that's a savings of $164. Pyramid that amount and the annual savings are substantial.

2. Consider the effective interest cost of **taking** or **not taking** a discount. If the amount that would be earned on the available cash during the time that payment is delayed is less than the amount of the discount, **don't delay payment**. The effective interest cost when you **don't** take a discount can be computed by using the following formula:

Effective		Rate of Discount
Cost (%)	= 365 X	Number of days payment is delayed past the discount date

    Example: If a $10,000 accounts payable has a discount of 2% if paid within 10 days and payment is not made for 30 days (delayed 20 days), the effective interest cost to you is 36.5%.

3. Take advantage of opportunities for special deals offered by suppliers (for example, installment payments, consignment sales, or special terms for purchasing seasonal merchandise that you can store for a few months).
    Reasons: Taking advantage of these "special deals" can greatly increase your gross profit margin and lower inventory risk. You also may be able to arrange with the supplier to delay a payment until the goods are sold. This is an especially viable option if the supplier is carrying a large inventory.

4. Avoid inventory overbuying. Excess inventory not only ties up cash but the holding charges (warehouse space, insurance, spoilage, theft, etc.) can easily add up to 20% of the value of the goods. In addition, the tax requirements to capitalize certain inventory costs makes excess inventories even more costly.

5. If the price and quality are comparable, consider purchasing goods and supplies from the fastest supplier. That can help reduce on-hand inventory. In addition, don't use too many different suppliers for a single item. If you order infrequently, they may not extend credit and the average price per unit may be higher. A supplier who knows he's getting all of your business on a particular product also may be willing to give you a better price.

6. If you're an important customer, ask the supplier to bill you at the end of each month. That will enable you to stretch out your accounts payable a few extra weeks without incurring any charges.

    Advisory: It's smart to delay paying suppliers, but don't abuse it. They may decide to make you pay in advance or consider charging you more.

7. Try to negotiate price discounts with your suppliers for large-volume purchases. Be sure to compare these savings with your inventory holding costs (i.e., warehouse space and the tie-up of your money).

8. Avoid overpayment of corporate estimated income taxes. You can usually get by with paying 90% of your estimated taxes or 100% of last year's taxes. Compute and pay the lesser amount.

9. Don't automatically pay sales tax. The sales tax laws vary from state to state. However, many states exempt from taxation goods that are to be resold, either in their present form or as part of a finished product. Some states also exempt machinery and equipment used in the production process.

    Advisory: In many states, the details of the law are complex. Don't rely on the vendor (your supplier) to determine if state tax is applicable. In most cases, the vendor is required to charge the tax unless told otherwise. Make sure you understand the basic rules for the product you're buying. Know what's taxable and what's not. If you don't, you could be overpaying for your goods.

10. Consider other income tax deferral techniques, such as: (1) the simplified LIFO method of inventory valuation, (2) the installment method of reporting sales, and (3) the completed-contract method of accounting for long-term contracts.

    Advisory: Check with your accountant on the last two items. Recent tax legislation imposed some restrictions on their use.

Ways To Manage Cash Balances

Managing cash balances to provide enough cash to meet the demands of the business, while minimizing idle cash balances, is a much-overlooked tool for proper cash flow management. Consider these techniques:

1. Use a cash management system that provides information on daily balances and automatically invests (even overnight) amounts in excess of state minimum balances.

2. Try to maintain a near-zero balance in non-interest bearing and check-writing accounts.

3. Transfer immediately (by wire) lockbox collections to the company's central bank.

4. Capitalize on the float by timing the movement of cash (from a money market or other account) with the payment of invoices, particularly large cash disbursements.

5. Open all mail immediately and try to deposit checks on a daily basis. You don't have to wait for the bookkeeper to post receipt of checks; they can be copied for later posting.

6. Talk to your bank about its cash management services. Many banks already have lockbox services and computer programs to facilitate the movement of cash.

   In addition, some banks have total cash and money management services. Your treasurer or comptroller should look into the various programs that are available.

   Advisory: If you're keeping the balance in your checking account low and you don't have overdraft privileges, be sure you know the balance at all times. If your bank has an on-line computer service where you can check your balances, whenever and as frequently as you choose, consider using that service.

7. Control cash advances to employees. Let them use their own credit card for travel and entertainment. Make them account for advances promptly.

8. Consider paying employees bi-monthly instead of weekly. That will not only allow you to delay paying the wages; it will also delay payment of your portion of FICA and FUTA taxes.

9. Project capital needs: Determine short- and long-term cash needs and prepare a monthly projected cash-flow statement. These projections will help inform you of the balances available for investment and any cash shortages that will

require financing or the movement of cash from money market accounts (or CDs) to your checking accounts.

Profitmover's collect fast and manage cash!

Be In The "Preferred Position".

Have Positive Cash Flow!

Chapter Twenty-Three

How Is Your Cash Flow?

Cash is KING! When you have cash and you work at using it properly, you are in what I call the *Preferred Position*. Most companies I've worked for are cash poor - continually fighting to make ends meet and certainly not in the *Preferred Position*. Invariably, they have no plan to fix this cash situation other than a general goal to make more profit. Good profits will help cash flow, but it isn't the total answer to attaining the *Preferred Cash Position Goal*.

To improve cash flow requires the development of a strong cash management system. And it starts with developing a cash flow projection. A cash flow projection in my opinion is the most important financial planning and analysis tool available to you. In fact, if I were limited to only one financial statement (which isn't the case) the cash flow statement would be my first choice. It tells me what my revenues are, what my expenses are, what my profits are, and most importantly, do I have enough cash to make everything work?

So what does a cash flow analysis tell you? It shows you:
1.	How much cash your company will need
2.	When you will need it
3.	Whether you need to look for outside financing
4.	Where the cash is coming from

There is an example of a cash flow worksheet on page 113. I cannot emphasize strongly enough how important it is for a company to develop this kind of financial analysis so eventually it can reach the *Preferred Position* - and not have to depend on borrowing money.

A cash flow analysis is necessary to budget the cash needs of a business and to show how your cash will flow in and out of your business month-to-month and year-to-date. It will emphasize when and how much money is coming in and going out so you will know and understand when you need to borrow money. Another advantage of developing a cash flow projection for the future (i.e., a year) is that it allows you to see clearly the effects of borrowing from a lending institution. This will help you focus on how to not only eliminate the loan, but even consider refinancing at a lower interest rate whenever possible.

Chapter Twenty Three

    Profitmover's understand and use cash flow projection because they know the importance of being in the *Preferred Position* cash-wise which means more profit.

PRO FORMA PROFIT PLAN AND CASH BUDGET (000')

PROFIT PLAN	Jan	Feb	Mar	Apr	May	Jun	Jul	Aug	Sep	Oct	Nov	Dec	Total
1. **Revenue**													
2. Variable Expense													
3. **Contribution Margin**													
4. Fixed Expense													
5. Depreciation													
6. Total Fixed Expense													
7. **Operating Profit** (3 minus 6)													
8. Other Income (Expense) Net													
9. **Net Profit Before Tax**													
10. Income Tax													
11. **Net Profit After Tax**													
CASH BUDGET													
12. **Cash Balance Beginning**													
13. Cash Sales													
14. Accounts Rec. Collection													
15. Other Income													
16. **Total Cash Available**													
17.													
18. Variable Expense													
19. Fixed Expense													
20. Equipment													
21. Taxes													
22. Interest													
23.													
24.													
25. **Total Disbursements**													
26.													
27. **Cash Surplus** (Deficit)(17 minus 26)													
28. Minimum Cash Desired													
29. Bank Loan Required Short-term													
30. Bank Loan Repaid Short-term													
31. **Cash Balance Ending**													
32. Cumulative Bank Loan Short-term													
33.													

A Good Plan is Like a Road Map:
It Shows the Final Destination
and Usually Marks
the Best Way to Get There

— H. Stanley Judd

Chapter Twenty Four

Do You Budget?

If you don't budget, then you probably do not have a business plan in place other than what's in your head, which is what you hope will happen. Most companies fail because there is no plan or process of analysis in place that requires accountability. When this happens most businesses perform poorly and more than likely will eventually close their doors.

You must have a plan (i.e. budget) in place that establishes the financial goals and standards you want to have happen in your business for success to be a reality. When this is in place a comparison against your financial goals and actual results can be done monthly. This is commonly called *Budget Deviation Analysis (BDA).*

BDA will allow you to have direct control of your business, but only if you will take time each month to use it. BDA will help you increase revenues, hold down cost and increase profits if you will spend a couple hours at the close of each month to understand the deviation and make changes so you get back on budget. BDA is the best financial source of current information you can have. The big question is, "Will you use it?"

Creating and using a year-to-date (YTD) BDA also will give you good financial information. From time-to-time expenditures can be higher in one month and lower the next. When this happens, the YTD BDA helps level out these swings. When you use the YTD BDA with the monthly BDA you'll have a better grasp of your operations.

As you become familiar with using and studying your BDAs, your budgeting will become more accurate which will help to direct your company to forecasted profits.

For your convenience, you will find on pages 116-117, two different budget formats. One is for the month and one is for YTD. Each shows the actual budget for the month, dollar deviation and a percent of increase or decrease. These budget formats are examples only. When setting up your own formats, get together with your controller and CPA for the purpose of establishing the budget format and nomenclature that fits your industry. This will make it easier for you to read each month.

When you look at these formats line by line each month you are managing your business the right way - the *Profitmover* way.

Profitmover's always plan by budgeting!

Budget Deviation Analysis (BDA) by Month

From the Income Statement
For the Month of

	A Actual For Month	B Budget For Month	C Deviation (B-A)	D % Deviation (C/B x 100)
Sales				
Less Cost of Goods				
Gross Profit on Sales				
Operating Expenses:				
Variable Expenses				
Sales Salaries (commissions)				
Advertising				
Miscellaneous Variable				
Total Variable Expenses				
Utilities				
Salaries				
Payroll Taxes and Benefits				
Office Supplies				
Insurance				
Maintenance and Cleaning				
Legal and Accounting				
Delivery				
Licenses				
Boxes, Paper, etc.				
Telephone				
Miscellaneous				
Depreciation				
Interest				
Total Fixed Expenses				
Total Operating Expenses				
Net Profit (Before Tax)				
Tax Expense				
Net Profit (After Tax)				

Budget Deviation Analysis (BDA) Year-to-Date

From the Income Statement
Year-to-Date

	A Actual Year-to-Date	B Budget Year-to-Date	C Deviation (B-A)	D % Deviation (C/B x 100)
Sales				
Less Cost of Goods				
Gross Profit on Sales				
Operating Expenses:				
Variable Expenses				
Sales Salaries (commissions)				
Advertising				
Miscellaneous Variable				
Total Variable Expenses				
Utilities				
Salaries				
Payroll Taxes and Benefits				
Office Supplies				
Insurance				
Maintenance and Cleaning				
Legal and Accounting				
Delivery				
Licenses				
Boxes, Paper, etc.				
Telephone				
Miscellaneous				
Depreciation				
Interest				
Total Fixed Expenses				
Total Operating Expenses				
Net Profit (Before Tax)				
Tax Expense				
Net Profit (After Tax)				

Calculations: A. Add current month actual to last month's year-to-date analysis.

B. Add current month budget to last month's year-to-date analysis

Understanding Balance Sheet Ratios
Will Lead You
to Making
Better Financial Decisions
for Your Company!

Chapter Twenty Five

Are Financial Ratios Important
To Running Your Business?

The answer to the above question is a definite yes!

I have discovered that most managers do not spend the time required to analyze their balance sheet. Most go to the final page of a computer run to see if they made a profit or not and that is as far as they go in their review. If they made money they say "Good", and if they lost money they say, "We have got to work harder." Not very scientific. Learning how to use your monthly financial information will help you determine what changes need to take place so better profits are obtained.

There are four general financial categories that should be measured.

- Solvency
- Safety
- Profitability
- Asset Management

By learning how to analyze your balance sheet and profit and loss statements, you will be able to determine the financial progress of your business, or lack of it, on a timely basis. This analysis should be performed by your accountant or yourself each month as a new balance sheet and income statement is completed.

For your convenience, you will find on pages 122-124, the definitions for key financial ratios. It is recommended that you become familiar with these definitions so that periodically you can determine good and bad trends in your business and correct the bad ones before much damage is done.

Also you will find a worksheet on page 120 and a Financial Ratio Analysis on page 121. By using the definitions and equations shown on pages 122-124, you can develop statistics that will properly measure your company against past results, industry averages and Robert Morris Associates (your banker's measuring stick).*

Profitmover's analyze their balance sheet on a regular basis.

---

* Robert Morris Associates (RMA) Annual Statement Studies RMA's Customer Care 800-677-7621

WORKSHEET

1. Current Ratio:
   Current assets $ _____ ÷ current liabilities $ _____ = _____

2. Quick Ratio:
   Cash $ _____ + A/R $ _____ = $ _____ ÷ current liabilities
   $ _____ = _____

3. Debt to Worth:
   Total Liabilities $ _____ ÷ net worth $ _____ = _____

4. Operating Ratio:
   Operating expenses $ _____ ÷ operating revenues $ _____ = _____

5. Net Profit Margin:
   Net profit before tax $ _____ ÷ total revenue $ _____ = _____

6. Sales to Assets:
   Total revenue $ _____ ÷ total assets $ _____ = _____

7. Return on Assets:
   Net profit before tax $ _____ ÷ total assets $ _____ = _____

8. Return on Investment:
   Net profit before tax $ _____ ÷ net worth $ _____ = _____

9. Account Receivable Turnover:
   Revenue $ _____ ÷ accounts receivable $ _____ = _____

10. Accounts Receivable Days Outstanding:
    Number of days in period _____ ÷ accounts receivable turnover _____ = _____

DATE _____

FINANCIAL
RATIO ANALYSIS WORKSHEET

	Current Month	Previous Month	Previous Year	RMA**	Industry

SOLVENCY

1. Current Ratio: Current Assets
                            Current Liabilities

2. Quick Ratio: Cash + A/R
                          Current Liabilities

SAFETY

3. Debt to Worth: Total Liabilities
                              Net Worth

PROFITABILITY

4. Operating Ratio: Operating Expense
                              Operating Revenue

5. Net Profit   N P B T*
    Margin: Total Revenue

ASSET MANAGEMENT

6. Sales to   Total Revenue
    Assets: Total Assets

7. Return on   N P B T *
    Assets: Total Assets

8. Return on   N P B T *
    Investment: Net Worth

9. A/R Turnover: Revenue
                                A/R

10. A/R Days: Days
                            A/R Turn

*Net Profit Before Taxes
**Refers to the Robert Morris Associates'
Annual Statement Studies

Definitions For Key Financial Ratios

1. ***CURRENT RATIO:*** Measures how much money is available in current assets to pay current liabilities. Current assets are those that can be turned into cash within one year, such as accounts receivable and inventory. Current liabilities are those that are due within one year.

   $$\text{Current Ratio} = \frac{\text{Current Assets}}{\text{Current Liabilities}}$$

   This ratio indicates the degree to which current assets are available to pay current obligations. It is a test for solvency.

2. ***QUICK RATIO:*** Measures how much is available in very liquid assets to meet current liabilities. The Quick Ratio focuses on cash and accounts receivable because they are more liquid than inventory and other current assets.

   $$\text{Quick Ratio} = \frac{\text{Cash} + \text{Accounts Receivable}}{\text{Current Liabilities}}$$

   This is a more stringent test for solvency and is a good indicator of liquidity. Since inventory and other current assets are not readily available to pay current liabilities, they are excluded from this ratio.

3. ***SAFETY RATIO:*** Defined as the ability of the firm to withstand adversity. It reflects the riskiness of the firm. It is measured by comparing total liabilities (debt) to net worth. This indicates the amount of money invested by creditors (debt) against the amount of funds invested by owners (net worth).

   $$\text{Debt to Worth Ratio} = \frac{\text{Total Debt}}{\text{Net Worth}}$$

   This ratio can be very important in indicating the safety of the business. Generally speaking, the higher the Debt Worth Ratio is, the less safe the business is.

4. ***OPERATING RATIO:*** The percentage of operating cost to operating revenue. This ratio shows whether or not the company is operating at a level efficient enough to leave profit after paying and amortizing all expenses against total revenue.

$$\text{Operating Ratio} = \frac{\text{Operating Expenses}}{\text{Operating Revenues}}$$

5. ***NET PROFIT MARGIN RATIO:*** The percentage of sales dollars left after deducting all expenses except income tax.

$$\text{Net Profit Margin Ratio} = \frac{\text{Net Profit before tax}}{\text{Sales}}$$

This is also called "Return on Sales" and demonstrates what percentage of the sales dollar is net profit before taxes. It is calculated before income tax because tax rates can vary from company to company, making comparison on an after-tax basis much more difficult. Again, the trend analysis and industry comparisons are very important.

6. ***SALES TO ASSETS RATIO:*** Measures the overall productiveness of the assets employed to generate sales.

$$\text{Sales to Assets} = \frac{\text{Sales}}{\text{Total Assets}}$$

This ratio indicates whether the assets employed in the business are generating sufficient sales.

7. ***RETURN ON ASSET RATIO:*** Measures how efficiently profits are being generated from the assets employed in the business.

$$\text{Return on Assets} = \frac{\text{Net Profit before taxes}}{\text{Total Assets}}$$

This ratio indicates whether there are excess assets in the business and if the assets are producing sufficient net profits.

8. ***RETURN ON INVESTMENT RATIO:*** The percent of return on funds invested by the owner(s) for a business, i.e., net worth (also called owner's equity).

$$\text{Return on Investment} = \frac{\text{Net Profit before tax}}{\text{Net Worth}}$$

Comparing a company's return on investment to the return of alternate investments, such as savings accounts, bonds, stocks, etc., will help an owner decide whether the business is a sound investment based on its relative risk level.

9. ***ACCOUNTS RECEIVABLE RATIOS:*** These ratios, analyzing how well accounts receivable are being managed, are called Accounts Receivable Turnover and Accounts Receivable Collection Period (ARCP)

$$\text{Accounts Receivable Turnover} = \frac{\text{Sales}}{\text{Accounts Receivable}}$$

$$\text{ARCP} = \frac{\text{\# of Days in Period*}}{\text{Accts. Receivable Turnover}}$$

These ratios help determine whether the accounts receivable are in line with sales. If receivables are excessive, the firm's liquidity is impaired, which could lead to future credit losses.

* If the accounts receivable are being analyzed for a year's term, use the figure 360 in the ratio; if a six-month analysis is being done, use 180.

To be a ***Profitmover*** you must learn how to read your financial information so positive changes can be accomplished. Failure to do so will lead to mediocre results or worse.

*Know Your Break-Even
and You Will Know
How Much Revenue is Required
Before a Profit is Realized!*

Chapter Twenty Six

Do You Know Your Break-Even?

When I work with companies, I always ask "Do you know your break-even?" Most managers do not! They should, but they don't. For me it is quite simple. When I know what the break-even is, I then know how much revenue I need before a profit can be made. *Profitmover's* know what this number is and they work hard to develop enough revenue each month so a reasonable profit is made.

The following format found on page 128 is used to develop the break-even or the point of revenue where you can expect to start making a profit.

The example shown is for XYZ Company and is calculated as follows:

Step 1: Look at the income statement for XYZ Company on page 129. Please note that all variable costs have been so noted with a (V), for a total of $389,241 and fixed costs of $314,521 are left blank.

Step 2: Determine the variable cost as a percent of sales by dividing variable cost of $389,241 by total revenue of $713,032 found on the income statement page 123, line 5 = 54.6%.

Step 3: Next, determine the contribution margin ratio by subtracting variable cost of sales percentage of 54.6% shown above from 100% = 45.4%, the contribution margin ratio.

Step 4: Now calculate the break-even sales by dividing the fixed cost of $314,521 shown in Step 1 above, by the contribution margin ratio of 45.4%, shown in Step 3 = the break-even of $692,778.

Step 5: To figure the break-even in sales for a month, divide the break-even of $692,778, shown in Step 4 by 12 months = $57,732 per month.

These calculations mean that on an average mix of business, the annual break-even for XYZ Company was $692,778 and the monthly break-even was $57,732.

Profitmover's know their breakeven!

Company: <u>XYZ Company</u>   Date: <u>January</u>

BREAK-EVEN ANALYSIS PROCEDURE

Step 1: Classify costs into two groups - Fixed and Variable.
Fixed costs are those that will remain the same over a considerable range of sales.
Variable cost increase or decrease as sales volume increases or decreases.

Step 2: Determine the variable cost as a percent of sales.

Formula: $\dfrac{\text{Variable Cost}}{\text{Sales}} = \text{Variable Cost \%}$

$\dfrac{389,241}{713,032} = \$54.6\%$

Step 3: Determine the Contribution Margin Ratio

Formula: 100% - Variable Cost % = Contribution Margin Ratio

100.0%
<u>-54.6%</u>
45.4%

Step 4: Calculate Break-Even Sales

$\dfrac{\text{Fixed Cost}}{\text{Contribution Margin Ratio}} = \text{Break-Even Sales}$

$\dfrac{314,521}{45.4\%} = \$692,778$
Break-Even Sales per month

$\dfrac{\text{Break-Even Sales}}{12 \text{ Months}} = \text{Break-Even Sales per month}$

$\dfrac{692,778}{12} = \$57,732$

XYZ COMPANY
INCOME STATEMENT
Period Ending 12/31/XX

1.		*Total Revenue*	*$ 713,032*	
EXPENSES				
2.		Salaries	157,163	
3.	(v)	Wages	135,699	
4.	(v)	Payroll Tax	20,311	
5.		Salary Related	44,265	
6.	(v)	Fuel	11,691	
7.	(v)	Tires		1,814
8.	(v)	Vehicle Supplies		599
9.	(v)	Office Supplies		6,621
10.	(v)	Packing & Material Supplies	62,320	
11.	(v)	Repairs & Maintenance	38,728	
12.	(v)	Professional Service		6,633
13.	(v)	Advertising	8,417	
14.		Utilities	6,506	
15.		Communication Services	9,414	
16.	(v)	Tractor Rent	4,562	
17.	(v)	Purchase Trans.		20,611
18.	(v)	Selling Expense		24,887
19.		Depreciation	16,105	
20.		Rent		7,488
21.	(v)	Bad Debt	6,743	
22.	(v)	Dues & Subscriptions	5,770	
23.	(v)	Postage	1,430	
24.		Property Tax	14,223	
25.	(v)	Claims & Losses		18,648
26.		Insurance	22,777	
27.		Interest	36,580	
28.	(v)	Other	13,757	
29.		*TOTAL OPERATING EXPENSE*	*703,762*	
30.		Operating Profit		9,263
31.		Other Income	4,752	
32.		Net Profit Before Tax	$ 14,021	

(v) = Variable Cost

Order Control is a Must
for Proper Revenue
to be Invoiced.

Chapter Twenty Seven

Do You Have Order Control?

In my travels over the past fifteen years, I found that my first impressions of a company when I walk in the front door are quite accurate as to its financial condition. The tidiness of the office, the demeanor of the employees I am introduced to, and the cleanliness and order of the desks and work stations tell me a lot about the company and whether it is in trouble.

I will never forget one experience I had on my first visit to a company in Texas. As I walked in the front door I could not help noticing file folders stacked on the desk, under the desk, and in rows of milk carton crates. The further I walked into the accounting department, the higher the stacks became. By the time I reached the controller's office it was apparent that the company was in the midst of a big audit or their paperwork was completely out of control. After talking to the controller for a few moments my first impressions were right. The company was strangling in paperwork, signaling deep trouble.

When you lose control of orders and invoices you can have problems such as:

- Lost Revenues
- Slow Invoicing
- Poor Cash Flow
- Credit Problems
- Collection Problems
- Unhappy Customers

So what do I mean when I ask *"Do you have order control?"*

Order control means that every sale or transaction is assigned a number upon order entry, invoiced timely and accurately and is accounted for in a given accounting period.

If you have order control it:

- Accounts for all revenue in the proper period
- Finds missing papers
- Makes invoicing more accurate
- Speeds up cash flow
- Makes invoicing faster

- Stops batch billing
- Improves customer relationships
- Helps eliminate collection problems

Most companies today are using an order entry computer software system that assigns an order number to every order. At the end of a given accounting period it will account for all orders invoiced and not invoiced. You should find all the orders not billed and get them invoiced prior to closing your books. When this happens you will have order control.

Be a *Profitmover* and get order control!

*"When You Hire People
Who are Smarter
Than You are,
You Prove You are Smarter
Than They are."*

— *R.H. Grant*

Chapter Twenty Eight

Are You Hiring Right?

Many managers and executives pride themselves on their ability to "pick the winner" after a single interview. They feel they can rely entirely on one personal interview, as they believe that experience has taught then how to pick the successful employee and that any other methods used to select people are a waste of time. Not true! Statistics lead us to believe otherwise.

The turnover of employees in most industries is disturbing; in fact, it approaches the turnover of salespeople in the insurance and real estate professions. It is expensive if you add in all the true costs involved around the hiring and training of employees. Experience has shown that the preliminary interview should be used primarily to eliminate applicants. Personal interviews alone are an ineffective method of selecting new employees because the opinions of interviewers are too subjective and affected by bias and personal experience to be considered exclusively accurate in appraising potential abilities. Surveys have shown that the judgments of even experienced interviewers in selecting salespeople are of little value in predicting future performance of applicants.

Several types of interviews are used in selecting employees: 1) the preliminary or screening interview, to eliminate obviously unqualified applicants; 2) patterned or guided interview, to analyze and appraise an applicant's history and experience in respect to the abilities demanded by the position; 3) the cross-check interview for the purpose of comparing the judgments of several interviewers and minimizing bias and 4) the final employment interview. All four types of interviews have a place in a comprehensive selection procedure.

Preliminary screening interview - The purpose of a preliminary interview is to eliminate those applicants who are obviously unqualified for the job and to provide time for a more thorough examination of applicants who are better qualified. The preliminary interview also protects your goodwill as an employer by a courteous, cordial reception of the applicant and gives the interviewer an opportunity to describe the selection process to applicants who are worthy of further consideration. The preliminary interview is used to determine quickly, whether the applicant satisfies the basic requirements of the job.

The screening interview is usually conducted by a manager or owner, someone who is competent to make an initial judgment and favorable impression of an applicant.

The interviewer may reject an applicant, or describe the selection process of the job and opportunity.

    Employment Application Blank - The applicant who passes the initial interview is given an *Employment Application Blank* to complete and an appointment is made for a patterned interview with the manager, or executive who will make the final decision to hire or reject.

    I feel the screening interview is of utmost importance. Remember, it is a two-way street; the applicant is looking over and considering the opportunities to go to work for your company, and if he or she does not have good vibrations about the job, the company, or you, this person may eliminate your company as a prospective employer in his or her own screening process. Good prospects can be lost if a professional effort is not given in the preliminary screening process.

    Applicant Interview Questionnaire and Guide - A patterned or guided interview is a standardized interviewing procedure designed to improve the effectiveness of employment interviews by aiding interviewers in securing and evaluating the pertinent facts about an applicant's qualifications in an organized manner. A *Standard Interview Guide* (see pages 148-153 for suggested guide) is provided each interviewer upon which to record his reactions to an applicant. The guide suggests key questions to be asked the applicant to reveal his qualifications for the job. The guide, in effect, provides the interviewer with a conversational track to run on. The order of topics to be discussed follows logically the significant features of the applicant's personal history, so that the interviewer can arrive at a considered judgment of an applicant's fitness. All of the pertinent facts and the interviewer's reactions are recorded in the guide, as compared to other interviewers' opinions. The guide provides clearly defined standards by which to gauge a candidate's qualifications. Applicants are encouraged to talk and give information about themselves so responses to the questions listed in the interview guide can be answered. This standardized interview procedure minimizes the usual bias and prejudices of interviewers.

    Reference Check-up - Consultation with former employers is an important step in reaching a decision to employ a new applicant. This step may be taken at any time in the selection process, but I have found the best time is after the screening interview. This enables the interviewer to have this information available for the guided interview, and if there are any questions relative to past employment, it is best covered at this time. While character references often have questionable value, no one is better able to report on the performance and cooperativeness of an applicant than his previous employers and customers. What others do not say about an applicant may be of greater significance than what may be said in his favor.

Specific facts regarding an applicant's former employment are more significant than the opinions of a previous employer. The dates of an applicant's previous employment, the amount of earnings, the volume of sales, attendance record and the nature of the work described in the application blank can usually be accurately verified by previous employers. But the opinions of former employers concerning an applicant's initiative, cooperativeness, popularity, and personality may be colored by personal prejudice or bias and be of little value in appraising the candidate's worth.

The most effective way to contact former employers is by a personal visit or by telephone, because information about an applicant can be secured by either of these more promptly and completely than in any other manner. In face-to-face conversations, former employers will give information more freely and confidentially than in writing. Some executives hesitate to give information about their former employees by telephone because they do not know the identity of the person calling. This objection may frequently be overcome by asking the former employer to call you back at your expense.

A typical telephone inquiry may take place as follows: "I am Mr. Larsen of the XYZ Company. Mr. John Doe, who states that he was formerly employed by you, has applied to us for employment. Although it may not be your policy to give out information of this nature by mail, we wish to make a decision concerning Mr. Doe at once. We would appreciate it very much if you would make it possible for us to get this information either by telephone or, if it isn't convenient at this time, may I arrange to come by and talk with you personally?" (If the indication is that it is alright to ask the questions over the phone, proceed with the *Telephone Reference Check*. (See page 154 for an example.)

An applicant's former customers and personal references are valuable sources of information which should not be overlooked in securing facts about the personal qualifications, honesty, aggressiveness, industry, health and good moral habits of a candidate. Face-to-face interviews or telephone calls to customers and personal references of the applicant will usually be productive in developing significant data.

Personality Dimension Analysis - One of the primary problems in selecting employees is the difficulty of appraising the intangible characteristics of an applicant, such as mental ability, personality, sociability, aggressiveness, confidence, and other traits which are important and essential to success in a given job. I have personally used this method of analysis for a number of years and have found it to be an excellent tool in evaluating a prospective applicant for different positions. I can also attest to the fact that after using *The Personality Dimension Analysis*, the turnover of employees diminished greatly. *The Analysis* should be administered prior to the final interview. (See validity factor from page 156.)

Cross-Check Interviews - The selection of a new employee is so important that most managers are unwilling to make a decision on an applicant on the opinion of only one interviewer. Personal prejudice, bias, and individual preferences, which influence the judgments of interviewers, are minimized by cross-check interviews. The same procedures varies from two to five, with an average of three. Recently, a study of the number of interviews needed to select salespeople was made by a large life insurance company. It was found that there is a direct relationship between the number of interviews given a sales applicant and his future success in the business. Several interviews enable the employer to make a better selection and also put a prospective employee in a better position to decide whether he or she wishes to enter the business. (See Cross-Check Form page 157.)

Job Description - The hiring process is a two-way street. The applicant is seeking a job with a company that he or she is qualified for, can contribute to, make a living and be happy. The company is looking for an individual who has the ability and personal characteristics that will fit the position so he or she will be productive and happy.

With this in mind, it is then important for both parties to understand what the position you are filling is all about. The best and most professional way for this to be accomplished is to develop a job description.

The job description should be given to the applicant and gone over in detail after completing the patterned or guided interview, and only if the applicant appears to have a keen interest in the job and if the answers given in the interview process are satisfactory.

Job Offer - When you have completely gone through the hiring process explained previously, and have narrowed your selection down to one applicant, you are now ready to make a job offer. The professional way to accomplish this is to do it in writing. (See the *Job Offer* format on page 158.) This format obtains the information required by your payroll department, outlines a general job description, starting salary, starting date, probationary period, benefits and probationary review date. The job offer is signed by the party making the offer, as well as the new employee. The new employee is given a copy and the original goes into his or her employment file.

Covenant Not to Compete - Over the years I have found that a Covenant Not to Compete is a helpful agreement to you as a manager or owner. When hiring a new salesperson, or manager, you are interested in a long-term relationship with the candidate. All the expense and training that goes into a new sales hire, should result in a long satisfactory relationship. Also, the covenant gives you the protection of not having people learn your business, become familiar with your accounts and customers, then leave to go to work for your competition, taking your customers with them. Some people feel that a *non-compete agreement* is as useless as the paper it is written on. I disagree! My attorney indicates that the real test of a *non-compete agreement* is it's reasonableness. The agreement I have used over the years does not hinder a person from making a living in the same industry, or even in the city where your business is located. But it does limit an employee from directly or indirectly soliciting, selling and/or engaging in any like activity which is directed at securing or selling a customer who has a record of doing business with your company during the prior year. *This is reasonable!* A former salesperson can go to work for a competitor but he has to agree to call on only those accounts which have not done business with your company in the past calendar year.

I have enforced this a couple of times, and in both cases, was able to get salespeople to stop calling on accounts. This agreement really works best as a deterrent and places a big question in the salesperson's mind if he should leave, and in some cases will cause him not to. *I would recommend checking any non-compete agreement you may use with your attorney, as laws concerning its validity may differ from state to state. See example on page 158.*

Performance Review and Evaluation - A good management program has a system to evaluate personnel on a timely basis. The format found on pages 160-163 is used to evaluate the new employee after the probationary period has been completed. It is also used for future reviews. Care should be given to explaining how you scored each characteristic and why. If the employee is performing at a level that allows you to recommend that he or she should become a permanent employee, then sections III and IV should be completed and this information should be shared as well. The original copy of this performance review* is to go into the employee's personnel file each time a review is made. By using this review process each quarter, you are informing the employee where they stand and what each needs to do to improve. It is also a great opportunity to tell employees how well they are doing. When this starts to happen you are managing your employees!

To be successful in business requires having a strong, loyal work force. Be a **Profitmover** by using a professional hiring program!

* A description and review of forms is found on pages 140 through 142.

DESCRIPTION AND REVIEW OF FORMS

STEP 1 - EMPLOYMENT APPLICATION

This form is to be filled out by applicants who are applying for managerial, professional and technical jobs in your company. Be sure it is indicated to the applicant that it is important to fill out all the information requested.

Upon completion of the application, the company interviewer is to read over all the information to determine if the applicant is qualified for the position. If the applicant appears to be qualified, the interview is to proceed to Step 2.

STEP 2 - APPLICANT INTERVIEW QUESTIONNAIRE AND GUIDE

This form is a questionnaire and guide to be used by the interviewer to help assist in the hiring process; to determine information that will assist in the selection of a qualified worker; to do the interviewing consistently for all applicants; and help the interviewer to comply with EEOC requirements regarding discriminatory employment practices.

STEP 3 - PRE-EMPLOYMENT TELEPHONE REFERENCE CHECK

This form is to be used to check reference information by telephone. It is recommended that whoever does the telephone reference check be conversant and knowledgeable in how to properly develop reference material over the phone. Also, it is an excellent idea to stay with the same questions and format so there is uniformity.

STEP 4 - PRE-EMPLOYMENT MAIL REFERENCE CHECK

This form is to be used when there is time to check references by mail. Be sure to fill out the top of the form, sign, and send a self-addressed stamped envelope for mailing back to you.

STEP 5 - PERSONALITY DIMENSION ANALYSIS

One of the most important steps in the hiring process is to determine the level of mental aptitudes and personality dimensions of the applicant. This can be accomplished by using a *Personality Dimension Analysis*.

These measurements determine how a person learns, his or her communication skills, drive level, sociability level, closing ability, etc. By comparing these measurements to the requirements of the job, it can be determined how well a person's performance will fit into the job in question. If that information is passed on to the individual he can personally benefit and grow through an increased understanding of his performance characteristics. This understanding leads to higher productivity levels and reduced turnover.

STEP 6 - CROSS-CHECK INTERVIEW

This form is used by other employees in your company when they interview, evaluate and give an opinion of the prospective applicants. They should have all the materials and information that have been accumulated by the first interviewer prior to meeting with the applicant, so they have an overview of the background and qualifications. This *Cross-Check* interview can be done by more than one person, if the originating interviewer wishes.

STEP 7 - JOB DESCRIPTION

The example shown under step 7 should be completed and given to the applicant prior to the job offer. After the applicant has read the job description and feels comfortable with the job as outlined, then the written job offer in Step 8 is given to the applicant.

STEP 8 - JOB OFFER

This form is used in establishing the criteria for the job being filled, by developing a general job description. It also establishes the salary/commission and benefits that would be paid. The interviewer should have this form filled out in detail prior to making the offer. After going over this information in detail, and assuring that the applicant agrees to the terms as explained and set forth in the offer, both the person making the offer and the applicant should sign, giving a copy to the applicant and keeping the original for the employment file. Be sure to set up the date for the first review, after the probationary period is completed.

STEP 9 - COVENANT NOT TO COMPETE

This form is used to stop an employee from taking business away from you. I recommend that you have all managers and salespeople sign this agreement and place it in their employment file.

STEP 10 - PERFORMANCE REVIEW AND EVALUATION

This form is used to evaluate the new employee, after the probationary period has been completed. It is also used for future reviews. Care should be given to explaining how you scored each characteristic and why. If the employee is performing at a level that allows you to recommend that he or she should become a permanent employee, then sections III and IV should be completed and this information should be shared as well. The original copy of this performance review is to go into the employee's file each time a review is made.

STEP 11 - WARNING LETTER

This form is to be used when it is necessary to discipline an employee, whether it be orally or in writing. By making a written report of the violation it will serve as a permanent record of the action taken along with the employee's acknowledgement of the discipline. The original warning letter should always be placed in the employee's personnel file.

STEP 12 - EXIT INTERVIEW

This form is to be filled out by the terminated employee and supervisor. It will evaluate the reason for termination and give insight to management. This information and knowledge may enable the company to make changes which will affect and lower future turnover.

CRITICAL EVALUATION & HIRING PATH

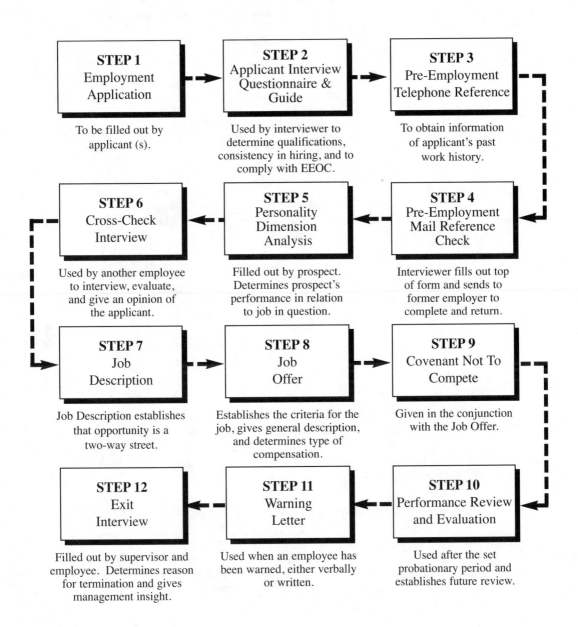

STEP 1
Employment
Application

To be filled out by
applicant (s).

STEP 2
Applicant Interview
Questionnaire &
Guide

Used by interviewer to
determine qualifications,
consistency in hiring, and to
comply with EEOC.

STEP 3
Pre-Employment
Telephone Reference

To obtain information
of applicant's past
work history.

STEP 6
Cross-Check
Interview

Used by another employee
to interview, evaluate,
and give an opinion of
the applicant.

STEP 5
Personality
Dimension
Analysis

Filled out by prospect.
Determines prospect's
performance in relation
to job in question.

STEP 4
Pre-Employment
Mail Reference
Check

Interviewer fills out top
of form and sends to
former employer to
complete and return.

STEP 7
Job
Description

Job Description establishes
that opportunity is a
two-way street.

STEP 8
Job
Offer

Establishes the criteria for the
job, gives general description,
and determines type of
compensation.

STEP 9
Covenant Not To
Compete

Given in the conjunction
with the Job Offer.

STEP 12
Exit
Interview

Filled out by supervisor and
employee. Determines reason
for termination and gives
management insight.

STEP 11
Warning
Letter

Used when an employee has
been warned, either verbally
or written.

STEP 10
Performance Review
and Evaluation

Used after the set
probationary period and
establishes future review.

EMPLOYMENT APPLICATION

We are an equal opportunity employment Company. We are dedicated to a policy of non-discrimination in employment on any basis including, race, creed, color, age, sex, religion, national origin, or handicap. Thank you for your interest in our organization.

PERSONAL INFORMATION   Date _____

Name _____
            Last   First   Middle

Present Address _____
            Street   City   State   Zip

Permanent Address _____
            Street   City   State   Zip

Phone Number_____ Social Security Number _____

Home   Own [ ]   Rent [ ]   Referred By _____

EMPLOYMENT DESIRED

                              Date You   Salary
Position_____ Can Start? _____ Desired?_____
Are You Employed Now?_____ If So May We Inquire Of
                              Your Present Employer? _____
Ever Applied To This Company Before? _____ Where? _____When? _____
Number Of Dependents _____

Education	Name & Location of School	Years Attended	Date Graduated	Subjects Studied
Grammar School				
High School				
College				
Trade, Business or Correspondence School				

Subjects of Special Study or Research Work _____

U.S. Military or   Present Membership in
Navel Service_____ Rank _____ National Guard or Reserves _____
Activities Other Than Religious (Civic, _____
(Athletic, Fraternal, Etc.)

Exclude organizations, the name or character of which indicates the race, creed, color or national origin of its members.

WORK HISTORY

Please provide information covering your complete employment experience, including time spent in the military service, if any. Be accurate and account for all of your time. Use the Comments area at the end of this section on Work History to account for any gaps in your employment.

Name and Address of
Company _____

_____

_____

Tel. No. _____

From Mo Yr.	To Mo. Yr.	Starting Salary	Last Salary	Reason for Leaving	Name of Supervisor

In detail, describe the work you did: _____

_____

Name and Address of
Company _____

_____

_____

Tel. No. _____

From Mo Yr.	To Mo. Yr.	Starting Salary	Last Salary	Reason for Leaving	Name of Supervisor

In detail, describe the work you did:

_____

_____

Name and Address of
Company _____

_____

_____

Tel. No. _____

From Mo Yr.	To Mo. Yr.	Starting Salary	Last Salary	Reason for Leaving	Name of Supervisor

In detail, describe the work you did:

_____

_____

REFERENCES: Give below the names of two persons not related to you, whom you have known at least one year.

Name	Address	Business	Phone No.

I authorize investigation of all statements contained in this application. I understand that misrepresentation or omission of facts called for is cause for dismissal. Further, I understand and agree that my employment is for no definite period and may, regardless of the date of payment of my wages and salary, be terminated at any time without previous notice.

Date _____ Signature _____

(EXAMPLE)

Job Description ***And*** ***Performance Standards*** ***For***	
Name:	Position: ***CONTROLLER***
Reports to:	

PERFORMANCE STANDARDS: List below the performance standards for the position. When employee is evaluated, rate the employee's performance against the standard by checking (X) in the appropriate column. Supporting explanations need to be documented on the back page if "BELOW" OR "EXCEEDED" is checked (X). Key standards should be identified with an asterisk (*) . Employee should be evaluated quarterly.

#	STANDARDS	BELOW JOB STANDARD	MET JOB STANDARD	EXCEEDED JOB STANDARD
1.	Direct and oversee all accounting personnel for proper productivity and accuracy.			
2.	Complete accurately all financial statements and information for all branches against budgeted figures, monthly and year-to-date by the 15th of each month.			
3.	Be responsible for collections, attaining a D.S.O. of 40 days or better and only 15% of receivables of 60 days.			
4.	Complete and analyze for each branch the ratio analysis for revenues, direct costs, gross profits, fixed costs and profit monthly and year-to-date.			
5.	Develop accurate cost of sales for each salesperson each month and year-to-date.			
6.	Develop cost analysis and maintain in concert with operations on all warehouse space.			

#	STANDARDS	BELOW JOB STANDARD	MET JOB STANDARD	EXCEEDED JOB STANDARD
7.	Develop, maintain, administer and distribute all cost areas			
8.	Develop and manage a zero base budget for General Administration (G&A)			
9.	Develop and manage a dated capital budget.			
10.	Develop, maintain and implement in concert with C.E.O, the following policies (a) credit policy (b) collection policy (c) bad debt write off policy (d) driver advances and statement reconciliation (e) payables policy			
11.	Develop, implement and maintain on a daily basis a cash flow analysis			
12.	Develop and maintain breakevens for all branches on total company			
13.	Measure and maintain standards/ratios as established via the C.E.O. or Executive Committee.			
14.	Develop and give at each executive meeting a financial report that gives the status of each branch			
15.	Serve as a member of the Executive Committee			

APPLICANT INTERVIEW
QUESTIONNAIRE AND GUIDE

INTERVIEWER READ THE FOLLOWING:

This questionnaire and guide is to be used by the interviewer and is intended to assist in the selection of a qualified worker. If it is used for all prospective applicants, it will help make comparisons for the purpose of selecting the most qualified applicant, and will provide objective information that will guide you in a professional manner in the hiring practice.

Remember: Federal Law prohibits discrimination in employment on the basis of sex, race, color, national origin, religion, and age. Care should be taken to avoid questions which indicate that any employment decisions will be made on the basis of such factors.

This Interview Questionnaire and Guide is general in nature, and some of the questions or items will not apply for all positions being interviewed. Skip questions that are not appropriate and substitute questions that are more appropriate for the specific position.

JOB INTEREST:

NAME _____ POSITION APPLIED FOR _____
1. How did you hear about this job (position)? _____
2. What do you think the job (position) involves? _____
3. Why do you want the job (position)?_____
4. Why are you qualified for it? _____
5. What would your salary requirement be? _____
6. What do you know about our company?_____
7. Why do you want to work for us? _____

If the above questions are answered satisfactorily, then provide the applicant with some basic information about the company and a general overview of the job. If a job description is available, this should be shared and discussed in detail, allowing the applicant to ask any questions.

8. Are you still interested in the position now that you have an overview of the job? _____

CURRENT WORK STATUS:

9. Are you now employed? _____ Yes _____ No. If not, how long have you been unemployed?_____.

Why are you unemployed? _____

_____

10. If you are working, why are you applying for this position? _____

_____

11. When would you be available to start work with us? _____

WORK EXPERIENCE:

Start with the applicant's current or last position and work back.

JOB 1

12. Current or last employer _____
    Address _____

13. Dates of employment: from _____ to _____

14. Current or last job title_____

15. What are (were) your duties? _____

16. Have you held the same job throughout your employment with that Company?
    _____Yes_____No

17. If not, describe the various jobs you have had with that employer, how long you
    held each of them and the main duties of each. _____

    _____

    _____

18. What was your starting salary? _____

19. What are you earning now?_____ Comments _____

    _____

20. Name of your last or current supervisor: _____ Ph # _____

21. What did you like most about that job? _____

22. What did you like least about it?_____

23. Why are you thinking of leaving? _____

24. Why right now? _____

Take a few moments and make any comments or general observations.

_____

_____

_____

JOB 2

25. What did you do before you took your last job?_____

_____

26. Where were you employed? _____

27. Location _____ Job Title _____

28. Duties _____

29. Did you hold the same job throughout your employment with that company? _____ Yes _____ No

30. If not, describe the jobs you held, when you held them and the duties of each.

_____

_____

31. What was your starting salary? _____

   What was your final salary? _____

32. Name of your last supervisor: _____ Ph #_____

33. May we contact that company? _____ Yes _____ No

34. What did you like most about that job? _____

35 What did you like least about that job? _____

36. Why did you leave that job? _____

37. Would you consider working there again? _____

If there is any gap between the various periods of employment, the applicant should be asked about them.

Comments or observations: _____

_____

JOB 3

38. Where were you employed? _____

39. Location _____ Job Title _____

40. Duties _____

41. Did you hold the same job throughout your employment with that company? _____ Yes _____ No

42. If not, describe the jobs you held, when you held them and the duties of each.

_____

_____

43. What was your starting salary? _____
    What was your final salary? _____
44. Name of your last supervisor: _____ Ph # _____
45. May we contact that company? _____ Yes _____ No
46. What did you like most about that job? _____
47 What did you like least about that job? _____
48. Why did you leave that job? _____
49. Would you consider working there again? _____

JOB 4

50. Where were you employed? _____
51. Location _____ Job Title _____
52. Duties _____
53. Did you hold the same job throughout your employment with that company?
    _____ Yes _____ No
54. If not, describe the jobs you held, when you held them and the duties of each.

    _____
    _____

55. What was your starting salary? _____
    What was your final salary? _____
56. Name of your last supervisor: _____ Ph # _____
57. May we contact that company? _____ Yes _____ No
58. What did you like most about that job? _____
59. What did you like least about that job? _____
60. Why did you leave that job? _____
61. Would you consider working there again? _____
62. Have you been unemployed at any time in the last five years? _____ Yes _____No
63. What efforts did you make to find work? _____
64. What other experience or training do you have which would help qualify you for
    the job you applied for? Explain how and where you obtained this experience
    or training. _____

    _____

EDUCATIONAL BACKGROUND:

65. What education or training do you have which would help you in the job for which you have applied? _____

66. Describe any formal education you have had. (Interviewer may substitute technical training, if relevant) _____

_____

_____

INTERVIEWER'S SPECIFIC QUESTIONS:

67. Ask any questions specific to the particular job for which you are interviewing. Write questions and answers below. _____

_____

_____

_____

_____

PERSONAL:

68. Would you be willing to relocate? _____ Yes _____No

69. Are you willing to travel? _____ Yes _____ No

70. What is the maximum amount of time you would consider traveling? _____

_____

71. Does overtime bother you? _____

72. What about working on weekends?_____

SELF-ASSESSMENT:

73. What do you feel are your strong points? _____

_____

_____

74. What do you feel are your weak points?_____

_____

_____

75. **Compare the applicant's responses with the information furnished on the application for employment. Clear up any discrepancies.** _____

_____

_____

_____

_____

PRE-EMPLOYMENT
TELEPHONE REFERENCE CHECK

Name of Applicant _____ Soc. Sec. No. _____

Name of firm called _____ Phone No. _____

Person talked to _____ Date _____

SAMPLE OF INFORMATIONAL QUESTIONS:

1. What were the dates of his/her employment? From _____ To _____
2. What was the nature of his/her work?_____
3. He/she states he/she was earning $_____ at the time he/she left. Is this true? _____ Yes _____ No
4. If "No", what were his/her earnings? _____
5. What were his/her reasons for leaving? _____
6. Would you rehire? _____Yes _____No   If "No", why not? _____
_____

How would you rate the applicant on the following characteristics?

	Poor	Average	Good	Comments, if any
Quality of Work	_____	_____	_____	_____
Quantity of Work	_____	_____	_____	_____
Attendance	_____	_____	_____	_____
Dependability	_____	_____	_____	_____
Overall, as an employee	_____	_____	_____	_____

_____

Signature of Interviewer

_____

Printed Name

_____

Title

_____

Date

PRE-EMPLOYMENT MAIL REFERENCE CHECK

TO: _____   Date: _____

_____

ATTN: _____

Dear Sir or Madam:

The person named below has applied for a position with our Company and has listed your organization as a former employer. He/She has authorized us to contact his/her former employers. We would appreciate confirmation of the information the applicant has furnished us about his/her employment with you, and also your assessment of the individual as an employee to the extent you can furnish it. Any information you provide will be held in confidence. For your convenience, I have enclosed a self-addressed stamped envelope.

We will greatly appreciate an early reply.

Sincerely Yours,

Signature _____

Name _____   Address _____

Company _____   Telephone _____

1. What were the dates of his/her employment? From _____ To _____
2. What was the nature of his/her work? _____
3. He/she states he/she was earning $_____ at the time he/she left. Is this true? _____ Yes _____ No
4. If "No", what were his/her earnings? _____
5. What were his/her reasons for leaving? _____
6. Would you rehire? _____Yes _____No   If "No", why not? _____

How would you rate the applicant on the following characteristics?

	Poor	Average	Good	Comments, if any
Quality of Work	_____	_____	_____	_____
Quantity of Work	_____	_____	_____	_____
Attendance	_____	_____	_____	_____
Dependability	_____	_____	_____	_____
Overall, as an employee	_____	_____	_____	_____

_____

Signature of Interviewer

_____

Printed Name

_____

Title

_____

Date

VALIDITY FACTOR ☐ Copyright 1994 Advanced Psychometrics Inc. San Antonio, Texas	C O D E	Psychograph For _____ Date _____ Company _____ Profile Score _____		
		LOW	**MID**	**HIGH**
ORGANIZATION By degrees concerning work and personal level of concern and planning need.	A	1 2 3 4 Prefers to let life happen as it happens. Details and planning considered unnecessary. Unaware of time constraints.	5 6 7 8 Organizational habits well formed. Limited structure accepted and needed.	9 10 11 12 Plans all alternatives before embarking on new projects. Needs highly structured environment. May over plan.
SENSITIVITY In relation to others and effect on personal emotions.	B	1 2 3 4 Thinks objectively. Does not let emotions effect decision making. May seem cold and aloof without realizing it.	5 6 7 8 Empathic, but not to a point of letting it interfere with emotions or feelings towards others.	9 10 11 12 Handling rejection or criticism difficult. May have emotional fluctuations often. Aware of how others feel at all times.
IMAGINATION How information is received and relationship to external stimuli.	C	1 2 3 4 Sensor. Receives all information through the five senses. Understanding of abstract or non-tangible ideas or concepts difficult. Lives in the present.	5 6 7 8 Good balance between two extremes. But still may have difficulty understanding abstract concepts.	9 10 11 12 Intuitive. All information received through intuitive sense. Understands abstract concepts easily. May lose interest when follow through required. Lives in future.
FLEXIBILITY Attitude towards rules.	D	1 2 3 4 Rigid. Personal outlook based on preconceived opinions and ideas.	5 6 7 8 Acceptance of new ideas and others' opinions easy. Objectively balanced. Will stand behind decisions, but also be open to others' suggestions.	9 10 11 12 Fluid thinker. Forms personal rules of conduct based on circumstances presented.
RECOGNITION Type of reward considered important and hierarchy of needs.	E	1 2 3 4 Needs regular salary and hours in stable work environment. Reluctant to take risks or change situations. Breaking of routine disturbing.	5 6 7 8 Needs regular salary and hours plus periodic bonus or incentive to augment base. Praise of achievements and efforts important to productivity.	9 10 11 12 Needs recognition for efforts constantly. Will take risks and gamble to achieve. Status important part of success.
TENSION Level of internal metabolism and effect on environment	F	1 2 3 4 Prefers fixed position in a protected environment. May seem slow to react, but can handle extreme pressure when necessary.	5 6 7 8 Good balance between two extremes.	9 10 11 12 Prefers frequent movement in unrestricted atmosphere. Constant routine disliked.
PROBING LEVEL Level of trust displayed in what others say and do.	G	1 2 Accepts others for what they say they are. Probing behind decisions considered unnecessary.	3 4 5 6 7 8 Will question moderately when faced with new decisions and rules. Healthy outlook concerning actions of others.	9 10 11 12 Others' actions questioned and probed for hidden meanings. Doesn't accept new information at face value.
SOCIAL NEED Need to interact with others.	H	1 2 3 4 Introvert. Prefers work which doesn't require interaction with others on a constant basis. May seem quiet and unresponsive.	5 6 7 8 Ambivert. Working alone or with others acceptable. May seemed reserved or shy since communication is transmitted on a need to know basis.	9 10 11 12 Extrovert. Needs continued interaction and communication with others.
ASSERTIVE How an individual reacts when challenged.	J	5 6 7 Submissive. May allow others to dominate in most situations to avoid confrontations	8 9 10 Can hold their own when challenged but may back off when a more dominant individual confronts them. / Uses assertive skills properly. Will stand firm when need arises.	11 12 Will attempt to tell others what to do and try to control situations.
COMPETITIVE Whether a person values friendship above a personal need to compete and excel.	K	1 2 3 4 Values friendship above individual need to win and excel. Will compete on a team for the good of the group.	5 6 7 8 Fairly competitive. Will solicit friends if they believe in product but will not always strive to win in all situations.	9 10 11 12 Oriented to compete and win in all situations. Constantly filling need to meet challenges and overcome them.
PROBLEM-SOLVING Skill in use in reasoning ability to determine relationships.	L	1 2 3 4 Can solve problems of a repetitive nature. May need additional time to render solutions in unfamiliar situations.	5 6 7 8 Good ability to solve problems. May need some review when encountering unfamiliar situations or circuitous data for the first time.	9 10 11 12 Excellent ability to solve problems. Assimilates new material at first exposure and deals well with complex data.
MATHEMATICS Measuring skills in adding, subtracting, dividing and ratios.	M	1 2 3 4 Mathematical skills limited to basic arithmetic. Allow ample time to assimilate more complicated mathematical equations.	5 6 7 8 Good mathematical skills. Should be able to handle everyday tasks involving arithmetic. New mathematical concepts will be assimilated in a reasonable period.	9 10 11 12 Adept at solving mathematical problems of a complex nature. When introduced to new tasks requiring numerical reasoning will assimilate data quickly and easily.
VOCABULARY Skill in matching word to its definition.	N	1 2 3 4 Vocabulary skills limited to accepted peer group. Effective communication with upper levels may be hindered.	5 6 7 8 Good vocabulary skills. Should be able to communicate thoughts and needs and adequately express ideas in oral and written form.	9 10 11 12 Superior knowledge of general vocabulary. Should be able to communicate thoughts and needs in oral and written form to peers as well as those in upper levels.
SPELLING Skill in identifying a misspelled word in a given group.	P	1 2 3 4 Spelling skills limited. May need additional time to review printed materials if accuracy required.	5 6 7 8 Good spelling and proofreading skills. Should be able to review printed material accurately.	9 10 11 12 Superior spelling and proofreading ability. Can quickly scan printed material and data with accuracy.

Printed by permission of: EVALU SOURCE, LTD.   Contact: Sue Laurent   Phone: 817-557-1272

CROSS-CHECK INTERVIEW

Date _____

Name of Applicant _____

Name of Interviewer _____

1. Do you have any questions to ask of me regarding the Company? _____
   _____

2. Do you feel you are qualified for this position? _____

3. Now that you have a better understanding of the job, what benefits do you _____
   feel you bring to this position? _____
   _____

4. When would you be available to go to work?_____

5. Do you have a valid Driver's License? _____

6. On a scale of 1 to 10 (10 being the highest degree of interest), what level of
   interest do you have in wanting this job? _____
   _____

7. How long do you feel we can expect you to work for us? _____

8. Do you need any additional information from our company for you to make ____
   a decision regarding employment? _____
   _____

COMMENTS: _____
_____
_____
_____

JOB OFFER

Applicant's Name _____   Soc. Sec. No. _____
Address   _____   Phone No. _____

_____
Position being filled _____   Job Title _____

_____
Date of Offer   _____   Person Making Offer _____

GENERAL JOB DESCRIPTION: _____

_____

_____

_____

_____

_____

_____

SALARY: $ _____   STARTING DATE: _____
PROBATIONARY PERIOD _____   DAYS*
BENEFITS: _____

_____

_____

_____

PROBATIONARY REVIEW DATE: _____

Offer Made By _____
Signature

Offer Accepted By _____
New Employee

* A NEW EMPLOYEE WILL NOT BECOME A PERMANENT EMPLOYEE UNTIL THE
PROBATIONARY PERIOD HAS BEEN SERVED. UPON SATISFACTORY REVIEW AFTER
THE COMPLETION OF THE PROBATIONARY PERIOD, ALL NORMAL BENEFITS DUE A
PERMANENT EMPLOYEE WILL START WITH THE NEXT PAY PERIOD.

(SAMPLE)

COMPANY NAME

000 NOWHERE AVENUE
CITY OF WONDERS, U.S.A.

COVENANT NOT TO COMPETE

In the event that the company COMPANY NAME terminates my employment as _____ because of dishonesty or criminal act, or because of failure to carry out duties as a _____, or I terminate voluntarily, then the following will apply:

    The company has places of business in the cities of _____ _____. For a period of one year from the date of the termination of my employment with the company as _____, I will not, directly or indirectly, solicit, sell, aid or engage in any like activity which is directed at securing or selling business from any account, person or business who has record of doing business with COMPANY NAME during the prior calendar year.

For compensation and benefits received from COMPANY NAME while working as Salesperson, starting _____, I,_____, agree to the above.

COMPANY NAME
By: _____   By: _____
    James B. Larsen   John Doe
    President   Salesperson

Date: _____   Date: _____

*This is an example only. Any Covenant Not to Compete used by your company should be reviewed and approved by management and its legal counsel.

PERFORMANCE REVIEW AND EVALUATION

Employee Name _____ Soc. Sec. No. _____

Job Title _____ Date of Evaluation _____

Date of Last Evaluation _____ Evaluated by _____

EVALUATION METHOD: DETERMINE AT WHAT LEVEL THE EMPLOYEE IS PERFORMING BY MARKING THE APPROPRIATE SECTION RELATING TO PERFORMANCE CHARACTERISTICS OF THE INDIVIDUAL. THE LOWER LEVEL OF PERFORMANCE IS AT (1), WITH THE HIGHEST LEVEL OF PERFORMANCE AT (5). MARK APPROPRIATE NUMERIC CHARACTERISTIC ON THE SCORE LINE PROVIDED. AT THE END OF THE EVALUATION ADD UP THE CHARACTERISTIC SCORES FOR DETERMINING THE AVERAGE SCORE UNDER THE OVER-ALL PERFORMANCE AND REVIEW EVALUATION ON THE LAST PAGE.

SECTION I

(A) **Quality of Work:** Refers to completeness, accuracy and neatness of work .... ____
1. Requires constant checking, often produces incomplete, or poor work .... ____
2. Work must be checked, occasionally inaccurate, incomplete assignments .... ____
3. Work generally meets department standards for accuracy, neatness .... ____
4. Needs little checking. Work is consistently accurate, neat, complete .... ____
5. Needs almost no checking, work normally exceeds all standards .... ____
          SCORE.. ____
          COMMENTS_____

(B) **Quantity of Work:** This is the amount of work the individual consistently produces.
1. Generally does not meet minimum standards .... ____
2. Completes just about enough work to get by .... ____
3. Meets standards for production, maintains average output .... ____
4. Hard worker. Effective, does more than is require............................. ____
5. Consistently produces substantially more than is required .... ____
          SCORE.. ____
          COMMENTS _____

(C) **Job Knowledge:** How well does the employee know all of the duties of the job?
1. Lacks some basic skills or knowledge .... ____
2. Has basic knowledge but lacks understanding in some area of job.................... ____
3. Generally knows job but needs guidance, instruction .... ____
4. Understands all facets of job .... ____
5. Has completely mastered all aspects of job .... ____
          SCORE.. ____
          COMMENTS _____

(D)   **Attendance:** Has to do with absences, tardiness
1. Often absent without good reason, and/or frequently late for work .... ____
2. Attendance/tardiness is more common than that of average employee .... ____
3. Generally misses little work, usually on time .... ____
4. Generally prompt and regular in attendance, misses work only with
good reason .... ____
5. Rarely absent or late; always with good and acceptable reason .... ____
SCORE.. ____
COMMENTS_____

(E)   **Dependability, Reliability:** Employee's ability to perform without constant supervision.
1. Requires close supervision to assure job performance.. ____
2. Sometimes does not follow instructions, needs supervision to
complete tasks.. ____
3. Usually follows instructions. Completes tasks within time limits .... ____
4. Can be depended upon to follow instructions with little supervision .... ____
5. Merits confidence, follows through on all tasks, requires minimum
supervision .... ____
SCORE.. ____
COMMENTS _____

(F)   **Drive:** Measure the employee's desire to attain goals.
1. Puts forth absolutely minimum effort, has no real goals .... ____
2. Goals are set very low, little effort made to exceed them .... ____
3. Set average goals, puts forth enough effort to reach them.................................. ____
4. Sets high goals, strives hard to achieve them... ____
5. Sets goals beyond levels of others, insists upon achieving them .... ____
SCORE .... ____
COMMENTS_____

(G)   **Personal Appearance:** Neatness, appropriateness of dress, cleanliness, grooming.
1. Does not apply to this job.. ____
2. Often unkept, untidy, poorly groomed .... ____
3. Sometimes careless about personal appearance .... ____
4. Normally clean and neat, appearance is satisfactory .... ____
5. Carefully dressed and groomed .... ____
6. Excellently groomed, usually good taste in dress .... ____
SCORE.. ____
COMMENTS_____

(H)   **Personality:** The individuals personal characteristics, as shown in relationships
with co-workers, supervisors, customers, visitors, telephone manners.
1. Does not apply to this job.. ____
2. Personality often unsatisfactory, often has friction or problems with others...... ____
3. More personal difficulties with others than most employees have .... ____
4. Generally gets on well with others... ____

    5. Very good personality for the job .... _____
    6. Personality is outstanding for the job .... _____
                  SCORE .... _____
    COMMENTS _____

(I)   **Work Relationships:** Ability to work with others and adapt to change.
    1. Argumentative, blunt, discourteous, cannot accept change .... _____
    2. Seldom assists others, reluctant to "help out", has some trouble getting
       along .... _____
    3. Agreeable, works with others, tries to be a team member .... _____
    4. Works well with others, can take pressure, volunteers to help out .... _____
    5. Friendly, helpful, seeks to facilitate activities of department .... _____
                  SCORE .... _____
    COMMENTS _____

SECTION II

Over-All Performance and Review Evaluation: Scoring Method: Add up all the scores of each characteristic, them divide the total score by (9) which determines the average score.

Total Score of Characteristics (Add characteristic scores A-1)
Average Score of Characteristics (Divide total score by 9)

Score at Last Evaluation:
    Total Score of Characteristics
    Average Score of Characteristics

SECTION III

Comparative Analysis: Under this section, compare this employee with another employee who has similar training, education and about the same length of service.

    1. New Hire: Too early to tell, but performance is about as expected.
    2. Unsatisfactory. Performance is below standard in one or more
       significant areas of the job.
    3. Below standard, but improving (We suggest that you set definite
       goals for improvement, together with definite dates by which
       improvement is expected. Give the employee another evaluation
       at that time.)
    4. Average/adequate, meets the standards for the job, but needs
       some development.
    5. Above average: Consistently performs above the standards
       for the job.
    6. Outstanding employee.

SECTION IV

Development Plan for Employee:
  Needs Improvement

     1. _____

     2. _____

     3. _____

Strong Points

     1. _____

     2. _____

     3. _____

Plan to Improve Weak Areas

     1. _____

     2. _____

     3. _____

Timetable

     1. _____

     2. _____

     3. _____

Signature of Evaluator _____   Date_____

NOTE: THIS PERFORMANCE REVIEW AND EVALUATION SHOULD BE DISCUSSED
AND SHARED WITH THE EMPLOYEE. ASK THE EMPLOYEE FOR COMMENTS AND
WHEN NECESSARY A COMMITMENT FOR IMPROVEMENT.

Signature of Employee _____   Date_____

WARNING LETTER

Date_____

NAME _____ JOB TITLE _____

BRANCH OR LOCATION _____

SOC. SEC. NO._____ SUPERVISOR_____

VIOLATION:

_____	Dishonesty	_____	Carelessness
_____	Quality of Work	_____	Absenteeism
_____	Productivity of Work	_____	Safety
_____	Tardiness	_____	Substance Abuse
_____	Insubordination	_____	Appearance/Dress
_____	Other		_____

DESCRIBE VIOLATION: _____

_____

_____

Violation Reported By: _____

Warning Letter By: _____

EMPLOYEE'S REMARKS CONCERNING VIOLATION: _____

_____

_____

ACTION TAKEN

_____	Written Warning	_____	Suspension	From_____	To_____
_____	Oral Warning	_____	Probation		
_____	Other	_____			

DESCRIBE IN DETAIL CORRECTIVE ACTION TAKEN: _____

_____

_____

_____

Person preparing & delivering warning:

    Signature_____ Date_____

Employee receiving warning:

    Signature_____ Date_____

Original to Personnel File - Copy to Employee

JOB EXIT INTERVIEW

Employee Name_____ Soc. Sec. No. _____

Address _____

Phone Number_____ Supervisor's Name _____

TO EMPLOYEE: WE UNDERSTAND THAT YOU ARE LEAVING OUR COMPANY. WE ARE CONCERNED ABOUT OUR EMPLOYEE RELATIONS, AND WOULD LIKE TO KNOW HOW YOU FELT ABOUT WORKING FOR OUR COMPANY. IT WOULD BE GREATLY APPRECI-ATED IF YOU WOULD FILL OUT THIS BRIEF QUESTIONNAIRE. THANK YOU.

MANAGEMENT

I. **EMPLOYEE** TO FILL OUT THIS SECTION

    A. Why are you leaving? _____

        _____

        _____

    B. Last day worked? Date:_____

    C. What did you like about your job? _____

        _____

        _____

    D. What did you dislike about your job? _____

        _____

    E. Were you treated fairly by your supervisor? _____ Yes _____ Usually

    F. Did you feel your supervisor encouraged you and listened to your ideas?

        _____ Yes _____Usually _____ No. Comments: _____

        _____

    G. When you had complaints or concerns, did your supervisor handle them fairly?

        _____ Yes _____Usually _____ No. Comments: _____

    H. Were you compensated fairly for the work performed?

        _____ Yes _____Usually _____ No. Comments: _____

    I. Were you given too much work to perform?

        _____Yes _____ Usually _____ No. Comments: _____

        _____

J. Did you feel you were trained properly?

_____Yes _____ No.   Comments: _____

_____

K. Were you in the right position with our company?

_____Yes _____ No.   Comments: _____

_____

L. Would you be interested in telling the President of the company how you feel about the company and how it is running?   _____Yes _____ No.

M. Would you be interested in staying with the company if different arrangements could be made?   _____Yes _____ No.

N. Under what circumstances would you be willing to stay with the company? _____

_____

_____

O. If you have accepted another position, what kind of work will you be doing? _____

_____

P. Will you share with us who you will be going to work for?

_____ Yes _____ No

Name of Company: _____

If you have any comment or observations please use the space below:

_____

_____

_____

_____

Thank you for taking time to fill out this questionnaire.

Management

II. **SUPERVISOR** FILLS OUT THIS SECTION

Employee_____ Supervisor _____ Date _____

   A. What was the reason for separation?
      _____ Resignation   _____ Fired   _____ Layoff
      _____ Medical   _____ Retirement   _____ Other
      Comment: _____
      _____

   B. If the employee resigned, was it for:
      _____ Another job   _____ Going into business for self
      _____ Leaving the area ____ Going back to school
      _____ Other
      Comment: _____
      _____

   C. If the employee was discharged, what was it for? _____
      _____
      _____

   D. If the employee was laid off was it:
      _____ Temporary _____ Permanent _____ Other
      Comment: _____
      _____

   E. Was the quality of the employee's work
      _____ Good _____ Average _____ Poor
      Comment: _____
      _____

   F. Was the quantity of the employee's work
      _____ Good _____ Average _____ Poor
      Comment: _____
      _____

   G. Would you rehire this employee? _____ Yes _____No

   H. If you had the opportunity to rehire this employee would you want to retrain?
      _____ Yes _____ No.
      Explain what training would be necessary. _____
      _____

I. Did you have any supervisory problems with this employee? _____

_____

J. List the employee's strong points. _____

_____

_____

K. List the employee's weak points. _____

_____

L. Do you feel the company should try to salvage this employee? _____Yes _____No

If you have any comments or additional observations please use the following space:

_____

_____

_____

_____

All of the forms displayed in this and other chapters may be ordered from:
JBL Enterprises
P.O. Box 1032, Wilsonville, Oregon 97070

"An Investment in Knowledge
Always Pays
the Best Interest."

— Benjamin Franklin

Chapter Twenty Nine

Are You Training And Educating Enough?

The need for formal training of employees is being recognized as a must for a successful business. Today, an employee must have a comprehensive knowledge of his product and services, organization, policies, market, competition, plus a perception of the market conditions. To acquire this essential knowledge, he or she must be constantly studying to improve his or her proficiency. Training is now considered as essential as the education of doctors, lawyers, or engineers. This means that a period of specialized preparation, training and continued education is a requisite for a modern professional employee.

If you are hiring a salesperson he must become more of a specialist than ever before. He must be able to diagnose the problems of his customers and recommend profitable solutions. He must have a working knowledge of economics, marketing, statistics, accounting and even commercial law.

From a salesperson's standpoint, training makes it possible for him or her to increase sales and earnings, to win recognition, and to qualify for a promotion to a supervisory position. A trained salesperson gains the confidence and satisfaction which comes from knowing how to do his work well. Increased job security is another advantage of training. Pride in the professional status of the salesperson is stimulated by greater knowledge imparted in sound training.

From management's standpoint, training salespeople is an excellent investment: 1) productivity is increased; 2) selling costs are reduced; 3) a better type of employee is attracted to the organization; 4) the efforts of all personnel are unified; 5) turnover is reduced; 6) less time is needed to put a salesperson on a productive basis; 7) the ability of a new employee is quickly revealed in the training process; 8) supervision is simplified and more effective; 9) intangible losses created by the mistakes of untrained personnel are avoided; 10) fewer employees are needed because the ability of the present staff is increased; 11) staff is stimulated to increased production; and 12) customers are served more effectively.

In spite of these many advantages, a substantial number of organizations provide little or no training. They feel it is expensive and results are intangible and slow in materializing. Some people resist training. Trained employees are often employed by competitors at a loss to the company that did the training. They feel that education involves so many variables that it is not practical to train a person to deal with a complex situation and training takes too much time. The attitude of some managers towards training is that it is expensive and results cannot be proven.

Training a person takes from six months to a year and can cost from $20,000 to $50,000, depending upon the person and the position for which he is being trained. It is not surprising that many managers shirk their training responsibilities. It is, however, a proven fact that companies that invest in training are more profitable and successful, and less likely to go into bankruptcy than firms that don't.

Most executives who have developed effective training programs for their organizations are convinced that it is the true way to success. Today, preliminary employee training is the crux of an organization. There is nothing more important in management than the preparation, education and development of personnel. Remember, it's not the bricks and mortar that make the company, it's the well trained employees.

Development of a Training Program

Training, to be effective, must be a planned, continuous activity. If a definite, specific, organized program is not adhered to, the pressure of other problems will interfere and training will become a spasmodic, uncoordinated activity, and will fail to attain objectives. A sound training program should answer the following questions:

- Who should be trained?
- Who should be responsible for training?
- What information is needed by the new employee?
- What should be the content of the training program?
- What methods of training should be used?
- When should the training be done?
- Where should the training be done?
- What training tools are needed?
- What results are required or wanted?

The answers to these questions will obviously differ from one organization to another, but the results sought are primarily the same. In your overall business plans, training of personnel must take its rightful place for continued success.

Be a ***Profitmover*** and develop a training program in your company.

Quality is Never an Accident;
it is Always the Result
of Intelligent Effort!

Chapter Thirty

Is Quality Important?

The answer is YES! YES! YES!

After being in the consulting business for more than 15 years working directly with more than 700 companies, there are certain business criteria that stand out in organizations that show profit. One of these criterion is summed up in the word *"Quality"*.

Companies that work diligently at *doing things right the first time* are the ones that show it outwardly the minute you walk in. They set standards and benchmarks and do everything to obtain these goals. The cleanliness of the office, plant and facility are clear indications of a company that wants to and does things right the first time.

I was asked to give a workshop at a United Van Line Convention a number of years back, and, as I often do, I attended the opening session to get a feel for the theme and what was being exposed as the hot item to follow in the coming year. Bob Baer, the C.E.O. of United, was introducing a new program for quality awareness. It was launched to measure United Van Lines as a carrier, as well as its agents. He was strong and upbeat in his presentation and indicated that United was going to set quality standards that would make the van line and it's agents the best in the industry.

At the time he announced this new quality program, United was the third largest van line in the United States in market share. What do you think happened? Within a short period of time United moved into first place and has held that position ever since. In my opinion, the day Bob Baer made the commitment to quality through the best measurement program in the industry, United was on its way to being number one. Customers were told and shown where the company stood in meeting its commitment to quality standards. In fact, the majority of information that was measured was developed from a questionnaire that the customer filled out. Every customer received a questionnaire and more than thirty percent filled it out and returned their comments and answers. It wasn't long before the word got out that United and its agents wanted to be the best.

I relate this story as an example of what quality can do for a large company and its agents. But quality can and will help large and small companies to prosper and become more profitable.

Recently, I read a book entitled *Quality Is Free* by Philip B. Crosby. The first chapter in part one entitled *The Understanding* read as follows: "Quality Is Free. It's not a gift, but it's free. What costs money are all the unquality things - all the actions that involve not doing jobs right the first time." He goes on to say, "Quality is not only free, it is an honest-to-everything profit maker. Every penny you don't spend on doing things wrong, over, or instead becomes half a penny right on the bottom line. In these days of who knows what is going to happen to our business tomorrow there aren't many ways left to make a profit improvement. If you concentrate on *making quality certain,* you can probably increase your profit by an amount equal to 5 to 10 percent of your sales. That is a lot of money for free."

Crosby starts the first chapter with a question and then gives a definition as follows, "What does making quality certain mean?" His answer to this question is, "Getting people to do better all the worthwhile things they ought to be doing anyway".

I've quoted from Crosby's book because in my opinion it is one of the best observations concerning quality and how important it can be to a company if taken seriously. Just think what would happen to your company if you develop quality that gave you an additional 10 percent of profits to your bottom line. It's free!

Another noted expert on quality was the late, Dr. Edward Deming. His philosophy requires organization to produce products and services that help people live better. Providing those goods and services is the real reason an organization exists. By providing ever-improving services and products an organization develops loyal customers and when a company has loyal customers real profits are developed.

Dr. Deming helped hundreds of companies to understand that when quality is introduced costs are reduced, productivity is greatly improved and customer satisfaction leads to more profitable business. So why am I spending time in this book writing about quality? It's quite simple. Companies that do things right make money! Companies that do things right have employees that are happy and proud! Companies that do things right have loyal customers! If you do not have a quality awareness program in place, start right now. Develop standards and benchmarks for sales and marketing, operations, accounting and administration and management. Stress that you are looking for zero defect.

The last thing I want to say is that for your quality program to be totally effective requires top management to be a participant in the program, not just a supporter. For success to take place everyone from top to bottom must be involved.

To be a real ***Profitmover*** you must have a quality program that makes you the best!

A Proper "Business Mix"
Leads To
Better Utilization
Of Assets

Chapter Thirty One

Are You Watching Your Business Mix?

There are many reasons corporations diversify into other lines of business. Among them is protection of the profitability of another line of business. In other words, a company may choose to participate in a business which by itself, is marginally profitable, or perhaps even unprofitable if the addition of that line of business enhances the overall financial position of the company. A company may buy another business to offset the seasonality of its present revenues. By doing this it may be able to use the present infra-structure and assets of the company throughout the whole year, not just six months.

Cash flow might be another reason for diversification. Adding a company that has fast turnaround on receivables or a lot of C.O.D. orders, could help enhance the overall cash position from a negative to a positive position.

Some companies expand or diversify to protect market share so a competitor doesn't overtake them in sales and revenues in the market place.

All of the above reasons for diversification have merit if properly analyzed and studied, making sure that the end result will be a positive action for the company.

Remember this: "Big is not always Beautiful". In other words, just to diversify or add additional lines of revenue can have an adverse effect on a company. Growing too fast can cause a company to fail!

It is important that you ask yourself the following questions when you consider changing your business mix:

- Have I determined what the cash requirements are?
- Do I have the managerial personnel to handle this acquisition?
- What effect will this additional revenue have on the present infrastructure of the company?
- Have I determined by means of a conservative proforma financial analysis that this additional business will have a positive effect on my company?
- Are there qualified people available to fill the positions required for this additional business?
- Will the profits of my company increase?

Good ***Profitmover's*** find the answer for all of the above questions. They study and analyze all aspects of increasing their company through acquisition or merger.

*"A Knowledge of Men
is the Prime Secret
of Business Success".*

— *Darius Ogden Mills*

Chapter Thirty Two

Do You Have The Big Four Plus One Support?

A number of years back, when I was going to college, I took a course entitled, Business Management. I remember the professor talking about the importance of developing strong relationships with four different outside support people, those being your Banker, C.P.A., Lawyer and Insurance Agent. He said, "To be successful these four individuals are required because of their expertise."

I never forgot his statement, and looking back on my business career there were times when I needed to borrow money, work with my C.P.A. on a big deal, have my lawyer get our company out of trouble and make sure the liabilities that I faced were properly covered. I did what my professor advocated. I went out and interviewed these individuals and hired them to be my outside management team, getting their commitment to help my business prosper and make profit. The relationship, as well as their willingness to study and understand how they could help me and my company were invaluable. When you have this kind of support and guidance you don't make many mistakes.

My banker's commitment to me and my company was to meet and go over financials each month and in doing so he was always up to speed when I wanted to borrow money.

There were times he would say "You can't afford to obligate the company at this time." and I would respect what he had to say because he was totally familiar with what our goals were and how we should go about obtaining them.

My C.P.A. committed to analyzing our financials monthly to give advice and suggestions regarding lowering cost ratio comparisons and productivity.

My lawyer committed to meeting with me each month to discuss any concerns as it applied to issues that I might feel could cause a problem in the company. If we didn't have anything to discuss we would always have a great lunch, and I knew he was ready to fight for and protect our company because he understood it.

My insurance agent committed to meeting with me each month to discuss claims, training and potential liability. He was an Insurance agent who worked at developing facts and trends that could help our company be more successful.

I've added another professional support person (ie: plus one) to the other four. You need to find an individual who can help you on a continuing basis with your computer system and software. It is important that you stay on top of the changes taking place in the data processing world.

It took some time for me to develop strong relationships with each of these individuals, and it took time on my part to help educate each of them in the role I wanted them to play in my company. Once that was accomplished I couldn't wait each month to meet with them. Sure it cost me a little money, but it was well worth it.

What every business needs is to find and develop the Big Five. If you want to be a *Profitmover*, these five individuals can help!

Without a Daily Plan
You are Like a Ship
Without a Rudder!

Chapter Thirty Three

Do You Have A *Profitmover* Plan?

In the first chapter I wrote about being an organized *Profitmover*. In this chapter I want to focus on financial goals by using the information found in each chapter of this book.

Your business plan (i.e. budget) provides an outline of your financial goals. Unfortunately, most managers hardly look at it on a regular basis, or use the management tools available to keep on track. The budget is completed, usually prior to year end and the only time a comparison is made is when monthly financial statements are completed. In my book that's not good enough! That's why I designed the *Profitmover* Plan shown on pages 186-187. When you use these tools (listed by chapter and page number) every workday, it emphasizes and makes you focus on whether you're on plan and if not, it gives you time to make corrections and adjustments. Don't wait until after the month is completed, then it's too late for you to make timely changes!

Profitmover's look at their plan every day!

Month _____ Year _____

PROFITMOVER PLAN

Monthly Goal

Revenue	Direct Cost	Gross Margin	Fixed Cost	Profit
$	%	%	%	$

Actual Attainment

$	%	%	%	$

YTD Goal

Revenue	Profit
$	$

Actual Attainment

$	$

Chpt	Plan	Page	Priority Date	Start Date	Comp.	Ongoing	Comments
1	Are You A *Profitmover*	7					
2	Can You Pass The *Profitmover* Test?	9					
3	Am I Managing My Company Effectively?	15					
4	Can You Pass The Sales Team Analysis?	20					
5	Do Your Sales Drive Profitable Revenues?	25					
6	Do Your Salespeople Understand The Importance Of Selling Added Value?	27					
7	Are You Sure You're Pricing Your Products And Services Properly So Profits Are Realized?	31					
8	Are You Costing For Profit?	33					
9	Do You Know Your Allocations And Cost Accounting?	39					
10	Do You Know Your Cost Of Sales?	45					
11	Do You Know Your Overhead Costs?	51					
12	Do You Know Your Labor Costs?	57					
13	Are You Controlling Supplies & Material Cost?	61					
14	Do You Understand Risk Costs ?	65					

Chapter Thirty Four

Do You Have An Exit Plan?

If you are the owner of your business there will come a time when you will want to sell and retire. When this happens you will want to get the maximum amount of money for your business so you can meet your financial and personal goals. That's easier said than done. I have found that most owners never sit down and develop a plan that leads them in an orderly fashion to parting from their company until they are forced to, and then it may be too late.

Sound exit planning is a process which results in the owner leaving his business in an orderly and pre-determined fashion. A plan that protects the integrity and vitality of the company as well as fitting into a retirement program that meets your needs. John H. Brown, the author of *How To Run Your Business So You Can Leave It In Style* lists six steps in exit planning.

1. Establish exit objectives
2. Determine the value of your business
3. Convert the business value to cash
4. Transfer the business
5. Contingency planning for the business
6. Estate planning

Every business is different, so every exit plan will have differences. However, every exit plan will have common elements. To better understand what these elements are, you need to ask yourself the following questions:

1. Do you have a planned departure date?
2. How much income do you need to achieve financial security?
3. Is there someone you want to leave your business to?
4. Do you know how much your business is worth?
5. Do you know how to increase the value of your business?
6. Is there a plan in place that minimizes your tax liabilities?
7. Have you provided for your family's security and continuity if you die or become incapacitated?
8. Is there a plan in place to insure that the business continues if you don't?

9. Do you have an estate plan that demonstrates cash flow and will meet your retirement needs?

If you can answer yes to all of the above questions, you're on your way to a good exit plan.

For you to successfully develop a sound exit plan you will need the advice and counsel of different advisors, as follows:

- Find an insurance agent who is certified and trained in retirement planning.
- Find a lawyer who is familiar and trained to establish proper wills that tie into your retirement plan.
- Have your CPA look at and agree with the calculations as they apply to taxes, gifting and leaving your estate to others.

Exit planning should be a top priority for all business owners. If you don't plan, eventually the state and federal government will do it for you. You don't want that to happen! Don't wait, exit plan now!

Profitmover's develop exit plans.

Change is Required Every Day
for a Company
to Keep Up With or Stay Ahead
of Competition!

Chapter Thirty Five

Will You Change?

Change is inevitable and is required to be successful! Top management in most companies I've worked with resist change and from my perspective this resistance is a major reason for failure or mediocrity. First, the attitude becomes one of saying, "We have survived doing it our accepted way for the last 20 years, and it should be okay to do it the same way for the next 20 years." The second reason is that management is reluctant to make meaningful changes because they require adaptation to new ideas. Often, by the time they are introduced it is too late to benefit from them.

Every business, no matter what kind or size, goes through or in and out of three stages during its life cycle: survival, maintenance and growth. These three stages can change from time to time, depending on the economy, competition and management style. If management does not react quickly and properly to these challenges by making the necessary changes as they are needed, profitability will be limited or non-existent.

A few years back I read a book entitled *"The Renewal Factor"* by Robert H. Waterman, Jr. He is the writer who co-authored, *"In Search Of Excellence."* The first chapter is entitled "Renewal: The Challenge." He shows how to look at a business (and ourselves as business managers) through a different mirror in order to meet the critical challenges of change. The critical challenges of change are what most managers have a real problem with. They procrastinate and stall because they are afraid to make change.

No longer can you wait for change to happen to you and your company. To be really successful you must make meaningful and timely change as it is required.

To be a *Profitmover* "I will change by using the information found in this book!"

Are You Keeping Up
By Reading Information
That Will Help You
Run Your Business?

I found out very quickly that one of the best sources of information to help keep me up to date as a financial business consultant was to read business publications. Over the last 15 years many of the books I read are worthwhile to pass on. They've given me reliable insights, valuable information and I recommend them to you. They will help you immediately to become a real ***Profitmover***!

"Must" Reading List
For Good Management

Agenda; Michael Hammer, Crown Business

The Art of the Deal - *Trump in Action*; Donald Trump, Tony Schwartz, Random House.

Being the Best - *Living Successfully by Being the Best you Can Be*; Peter F. Drucker, Harper & Row Publishers.

Being the Best - *When the Self-Help Myths Leave You Empty and Hungry For the Truth*; Denis Waitley, Oliver Nelson.

Ben Franklin's 12 Rules of Management T*he Founding Father of American Business Solves Your Toughest Problems*; Blaine McCormick, Entrepeneur Press.

Beyond Survival - *A Guide For the Business Owner & His Family*; Leon A. Danco, University Press.

The Business Planning Guide - *7th Edition - Creating a Plan for Success in Your Own Business*; David H. Bangs, Jr., Upstart.

Buy Low, Sell High, Collect Early & Pay Late - *The Manager's Guide To Financial Survival*; Dick Levin, Prentice Hall.

Cash In On Cash Flow - *50 Tough-as-Nails Ideas for Revitalizing Your Business*; A. David Silver, AMACOM.

The Complete Book of Business Success; Byrd Baggett, Rutledge Hill Press.

Compensating Your Sales Force - *How to Use Salaries, Commissions, Draws, Bonuses, Perks, Contests, Territories, and Quotes to Motivate Your Sales Force and Increase Sales*; W.G. Ryckman, Probus.

Dig Your Well Before You're Thirsty - *The Only Network Book You'll Ever Need*; Harvey Mackay, Currency Doubleday.

Double Your Profits In 6 Months Or Less - *78 Ways to Cut Costs, Increase Sales & Dramatically Improve Your Bottom Line*; Bob Fifer, Harper Collins.

Dr. Deming - The American Who Taught The Japanese About Quality*;* Rafael Aguayo, Fireside, Simon & Schuster.

The Effective Executive - *Analyzes the Practices the Executive Must Master in Order to Be Truly Effective*; Peter F. Drucker, Harper & Row Publishers. Executive Essentials - The One Guide to What Every Rising Businessperson Should Know; Mitchell J. Posner, Avon.

Financial Essentials for Small Business Success - *Accounting, Planning and Recordkeeping Techniques for a Healthy Bottom Line*; Joseph Tabet & Jeffrey Slater, Upstart.

First, Break All the Rules - *What the World's Greatest Managers Do Differently*; Marcus Buckingham & Curt Coffman, Simon & Schuster.

Further Up the Organization - *How to Stop Management From Stifling People & Strangling Productivity*; Robert Townsend, Knopf.

Get Better or Get Beaten! - *29 Leadership Secrets from GE's Jack Welch - New and Updated Edition*; Robert Slater, McGraw Hill.

Getting It to the Bottom Line - *Management by Incremental Gains*; Richard S. Sloma, Free Press.

The Greatest Salesman in the World - *Part II, the End of the Story*; Og Mandino, Bantam.

How I Raised Myself From Failure to Success in Selling - *How to Develop Your Skills as a Salesman & Capitalize on the Skills You Already Have*; Frank Bettger, Prentice Hall, Inc.

How to Manage and Help Salesmen*;* Charles B. Roth, Prentice Hall.

How to Sell Against Tough Competition*;* Harry Kuese, Prentice Hall.

How to Win Customers and Keep Them for Life*;* Michael LeBoef, Berkley.

Insights Into Excellence - *Winning Game Plans from 19 Masters of Business Success*; The Members of Speakers Associates, HDL Publishing.

Jack - Straight from the Gut; Jack Welch with John A. Byrne, Warner Business Books

The Jack Welch - *Lexicon of Leadership*; Jeffrey A. Krames, McGraw Hill

Keeping the Family Business Healthy - *How to Plan for Continuing Growth, Profitability and Family Leadership*; John L. Ward, Jossey-Bass.

Lead, Follow or Get Out of the Way - *Leadership Strategies for the Thoroughly Modern Manager*; Jim Lundy, Avant Books.

Leaders - *The Four Keys of Effective Leadership*; Warren Bennis, Burt Nanus, Harper & Row Publishers.

Leadership and the One Minute Manager - *Increasing Effectiveness Through Situational Leadership*; Kenneth Blanchard, PH.D, Patricia Zigarmi, Ed.D, Drea Zigarmi, Ed.D, Morrow.

Leadership Jazz - *The Art of Conducting Business Through: Leadership -Followership - Teamwork - Touch - Voice*; Max Depree, DTP.

Leading Change - *An Action Plan from the World's Foremost Expert on Business Leadership*; John P. Kotter, Harvard Business School Press.

Liberation Management - *The Art of Caring Leadership*; Tom Peters, Knopf.

Love & Profit*;* James A. Autry, Morrow.

Making Six Sigma Last; George Eckes, Wiley Books

Managing - *The Legendary Super Manager Shows You the Inside Secrets That Guarantee Corporate Success*; Harold Geneen, Alvin Moscow, Avon.

Managing the Equity Factor *"or After All I've Done for You..."*; Richard C. Huseman, Ph.D, Houghton Mifflin.

Mastery of Management - *How to Avoid Obsolescence by Preparing for Tomorrow's Management Today*; Auren Uris, Playboy Press.

Memos from the Chairman; Alan C. Greenberg, Workman.

The Mentor - *15 Keys to Success in Sales, Business & Life*; Jack Carew, Donald I. Fine Books.

My Lifetime Treasury of Selling Secrets; Charles B. Roth, Prentice Hall.

Negotiate to Close - *How to Make More Successful Deals*; Gary Karrass, Simon & Schuster.

The New Managers Survival Manual - *All the Skills You Need for Success*; Clay Carr, Wiley.

Ninety Days to Financial Fitness*;* Don & Joan German, Collier Books.

No Bull Sales Management - *The Unbeatable New Guide to Running a Super Successful Sales Force*; Hank Trisler, Bantam.

Profit - *200 Sure-fire Ideas for Making Your Business Better*; Alex McKee, Key Porter Books.

Profit Dynamics - *Achieving Consistent Bottom Line Results*; John A. Tracy, Dow Jones Irwin.

Quality is Free - *The Art of Making Quality Certain*; Philip B. Crosby, Mentor.

Quality is Still Free - *Making Quality Certain in Uncertain Times*; Philip B. Crosby, McGraw Hill.

The Renewal Factor - *How to Best Get and Keep the Competitive Edge*; Robert H. Waterman, Jr., Bantam.

Secrets of Closing Sales; Charles B. Roth, Prentice Hall.

Secrets of Selling Yourself to People*;* James T. Mangan, Prentice Hall.

Six Sigma - *The Breakthrough Management Strategy Revolutionizing The World's Top Corporations*; Mikel Harry, PH.D., Richard Schroeder, Currency Doubleday

Strategic Planning - *What Every Manager Must Know, A Step by Step Guide*; George A Steiner, Free Press.

Success Strategies for the New Sales Manager - *Proven Techniques & Tips That Help New Sales Managers Past the First 200 Day Sales Barrier & Into Higher Successful Careers*; Mack Hanan, Howard Berrian, James Cribbin, Jack Donis, AmaCom.

Successful Cold Call Selling - *Step by Step Techniques to Help the Salesperson Master the Art of the Cold Call*; Lee Boyan, AmaCom.

Successful Small Business Management - *Planning & Control, Accounting & Financial Management, and Marketing and Sales*; Leon A. Wortman, AmaCom.

Successful Telephone Selling in the 80's - *How to Increase Your Sales Production Dramatically by Using the Telephone*; Martin D. Shafiroff, Robert L Shook, Harper & Row Publishers.

Swim With the Sharks Without Being Eaten Alive - *How to Outsell, Outmanage, Outmotivate & Outnegotiate Your Competition*; Harvey Mackay, William Morrow & Co.

Teams - *How to Develop Peak Performance Teams for World Class Results*; James L. Lundy, Dartmnell.

The Ten Commandments of Business & How to Break Them - *Secrets for Improving Employee Morale, Enhancing Customer Service, Increasing Company Profits, While Having More Fun Than You Ever Thought You Could Have at Work*; Bill Fromm, Putnam.

Theory Z - *How American Business Can Meet the Japanese Challenge*; William G. Ouchi, Avon.

The Turnaround Manager's Handbook - *How to Examine, Diagnose, and Treat Your Company Back to Fiscal Health*; Richard S. Sloma, Free Press.

What They Still Don't Teach You at Harvard Business School - *Notes From a Street Smart Executive*; Mark H. McCormack, Bantam.

The Winning Performance - *How America's High Growth Midsize Companies Succeed*; Donald K. Clifford, Jr., Richard E. Cavanagh, Bantam.

Winning Strategies for Managing People - *A Task Oriented Guide to Hiring, Goal Setting, Encouraging, Reprimanding, Promoting, Demoting, Stroking, Warning, and Firing*; Robert Irwin,Rita Wolenik, Franklin Watts.

Who Moved My Cheese? - *An A-mazing Way to Deal with Change in Your Work and in Your Life*; Spencer Johnson, M.D., Putnam.

You Can't Teach a Kid to Ride a Bike at a Seminar; David H. Sandler, Dutton.

Zero Base Budgeting - *A Practical Management Tool for Evaluating Expenses*; Peter A. Pyhrr, Wiley Interscience.

About The Author

James B. Larsen

James B. Larsen has been active in the transportation industry for 30 years in various positions. Starting in 1959, he became a truck driver hauling bulk oil product. A year later, Larsen accepted a sales position with a small trucking company selling transportation services. Within two years, he was promoted to sales manager and increased the company's sales by 600% with a commensurate increase in profit.

By 1962, Larsen had become a stockholder of Lile International Companies and was elevated to general manager of the company ten years later. He was later promoted to president and chief operating officer of the company, helping to build one of the largest diversified transportation organizations of its type in the United States. He resigned and sold his interests in the Lile Companies in May of 1982 to establish JBL Enterprises, a consulting firm specializing in the transportation industry. Since then he has been the top financial advisor to hundreds of companies that required profitmaking strategies and changes.

He has taught popular workshops nationwide on "Understanding Your Costs," "Pricing Your Services for a Profit," "In Search of the Elusive Dollar," and "On the Road to Profit." In addition, Larsen is the author of *Hiring For Success, Getting Results by Sales Planning, Costing for $$$, Where Are The Profits,* and *Profitable Roads Ahead.*

In his role as "turnaround specialist", Larsen has counseled such diverse entities as transportation companies (van lines, freight lines, agents, etc.), automobile dealerships, home security, general distributuion organizations, real estate developer, and U.S. government agencies. Larsen's expertise has been invaluable to numerous membership organizations and he has served as Board member and chairman, National Moving and Storage Association; Board member and president, Oregon's Dairymen's Association; Board member and president, Administrative Management Society; Board member and chairman, Mayflower Warehousemen's Association and as a member of the Board of Directors, Federal Banking Institution.

Other Books by Jim Larsen

Where Are the Profits? - Cost control for the transportation company. Case studies demonstrate how to make a cost analysis to determine profit and loss, gross margins and various ratios.

$ 39.50

On the Road to Profit - A study course for the independent contract driver and company showing how to determine, trace and control costs in relation to revenues.

$29.50

Starting Your Own Business - How to start and grow into handling office and industrial moves profitably; how to prospect. estimate, price and sell, equipment needs, as well as organization, billing an collecting.

$39.50

Excellence in Dispatch and Operations - Determining and understanding the responsibilities of managing the direct cost of workers, trucks and company assets to allow profitability.

$ 29.50

Excellence in Selling and Servicing International Moving - Methods to find international business, selling door-to-door move, developing commercial accounts, packing, loading, documentation and cost analysis.

$ 29.50

Excellence in Packing and Crating - This manual is about proper procedures for packing and crating household goods, materials used, packing methods, cost analysis, standards and measurements, and a packer's qualification test.

$29.50

Excellence in Record Storage - How to prospect, sell, price and store inventory, train personnel, develop a market study and perform cost and profit analysis.

$29.50

Excellence in Selling Moving and Storage Services - This manual deals with hiring, training, goal setting, prospecting and solicitation, sales planning, added-value selling, cost of sales analysis and sales management.

$39.50

For more information about the manuals, as well as consulting
and workshops on the subjects covered, contact:
James B. Larsen - JBL Enterprises
P.O.Box 1032 - Wilsonville, OR 97070
Phone: 503-682-7164 - Fax: 503-682-7807

Order Form

NAME: _____

COMPANY: _____

ADDRESS: _____

CITY: _____ STATE: _____ ZIP: _____

PHONE: (AREA CODE) _____

ENCLOSED IS MY CHECK FOR $_____
                              (U.S. CURRENCY)

QUANTITY	MANUALS	COST
_____	The Profitmover's Guide to Success $24.95	$ _____
_____	Where Are The Profits $39.50	$ _____
_____	On The Road To Profits $29.50	$ _____
_____	Starting Your Own O&I Business.......................$39.50	$ _____
_____	Excellence In Dispatch And Operations.............$29.50	$ _____
_____	Excellence In International Moving $29.50	$ _____
_____	Excellence In Packing And Crating $29.50	$ _____
_____	Excellence In Record Storage............................$29.50	$ _____
_____	Excellence In Selling Moving And	
	Storage Services...$39.50	$ _____
		$ _____
	Shipping & Handling	
	($6.50 each manual)	$ _____
	TOTAL	$ _____

✉ Mail to:
JBL Enterprises
P.O. Box 1032
Wilsonville, OR 97070

Make checks payable to:
JBL Enterprises

1. Allow 2 to 3 weeks for delivery.
2. Add $6.50 per manual for shipping & handling.
3. All orders must be accompanied by payment.

FOR CREDIT CARD USERS: ❑ VISA ❑ MasterCard

NUMBER _____

SIGNATURE: _____